CONTENTS

INTRODUCTION

Life on Earth exists in every far-flung corner – from the sun-beaten desert to the icy tundra of the North Pole. Animals have adapted to inhospitable environments and are able to survive in the most extreme conditions. Their amazing abilities to withstand heat, cold, the perils of the rainforest and the deepest oceans, ensures the continuation of the planet's most awesome creatures.

THE HOSPITABLE DESERT

The desert regions of the world receive very little rainfall – less than 25 cm (10 inches) a year. In some deserts, such as the Atacama Desert of South America, it never rains at all. Deserts are the hottest and driest places in the world, receiving the most amount of sunlight on Earth. However, even in this unbearably hot, dry environment, life is able to thrive. Cacti plants are able to store what little water does fall for long periods. Likewise, camels are able to store fat in their humps for their long treks across the desert. Through adapting to the hot, dry environment during the day, and the bitterly cold nights, these lifeforms are able to live where others cannot survive.

POLE TO POLE

The North and South Poles are the coldest places on Earth. Very little sunlight falls here, and in fact during the long winters, the Sun hardly shines at all. If you stood at one of the poles without any protection, you would be frozen solid in a matter of minutes. However, the Arctic is full of life during the short summer months. Seals, foxes, hares and bears all thrive on the icy landscape. Their thick layers of blubber or fur keep them insulated and protect them from the bitter cold winds that ravage this part of the Earth. In the Summer they breed, ensuring there is new life for next year's generation of animals.

LIVING PLANET

By Paul Bennet and Barbara Taylor

NATURAL WORLD

Life on Earth has been able to adapt to the harshest conditions; from the bitter cold of the North and South poles to the sweltering heat of the world's deserts. Not only does life survive in these inhospitable extremes, it has also flourished in the world's rainforests and oceans, producing an amazing array of colour and shape.

Acknowledgements

Copyright © 2006 *ticktock* Entertainment Ltd. First published in Great Britain by ticktock Media Ltd., Unit 2, Orchard Business Centre, North Farm Road, Tunbridge Wells, Kent TN2 3XF, Great Britain.

All rights reserved. No part of this publication may be reproduced, stored in a retrieval system, or transmitted in any form or by any means electronic, mechanical, photocopying, recording or otherwise, without prior written permission of the copyright owner.

A CIP catalogue record for this book is available from the British Library.

ISBN 978 1 86007 572 8 Printed in China.

Picture Credits: t=top, b=bottom, c=centre, l=left, r=right, OFC=outside front cover, OBC=outside back cover.
AKG Photo; 37rb. Andy Crump/Still Pictures; 69b. Auscape; 12tl, 25c, 32bl. B&C Alexander Photography; 4b, 8tl, 55, 36c, 36/37t, 37tl, 38tl, 38/39 (main pic), 39c, 40tl, 41br, 41hl, 42bl, 42/43b, 42/43c, 43br, 44bl, 44tl, 44cı, 46/47b, 46/47c, 48/49 (main pic), 49tr, 49cr, 50l, 52br, 52cl, 52tc, 52/53t, 56tl, 56/57b, 57c, 57tr, 58tl, 58c, 59cr, 59tl, 59/60 (main pic), 59/60c, 60tr, 62bc, 62bl, 62tl, 63bl, 63br, 63c, 63tl, 64l, 64/65bc, 65cl, 65tr, 86/87t, 122/123c, 123cr. BBC Natural History Unit; 26cl, 80b. Bruce Colman Limited; 16bl, 24bl, 28tl, 70bl, 90ct, 95tr, 106/107b, 108tr, 114tl. Colorific; 12c. FLPA; 23bc, 33tl. Innerspace Visions; 84/85b. Jacana; 96tl, 100bl, 101tr, 101br, 102cr, 104/105t, 105tr, 106tl, 107r, 108bl, 111tr, 112c, 112/113c, 113b, 115br, 120/121c, 121b, 125br. Michel Freeman/Auscape; 92/93ct. NHPA; 19tl, 22b, 25br, 29tr, 28/29t, 30tl, 30bl, 76tl, 88/89 (main pic). Oxford Scientific Films; OFC (c, far left), 4tr, 4t, 6tc, 6b, 6/7c, 10br, 8/9t, 8/9c, 9cr, 10tl, 12bc, 12lb, 12/13c, 13b, 14tl, 14bl, 14/15bc, 15c, 17tl, 18l, 18/19c, 19b, 19c, 21tl, 21r, 22tl, 22/23t, 24/25b, 25cr, 26bl, 26/27t, 26/27b, 27tr, 31cr, 35tr, 37tr, 39tr, 40tr, 42c, 42l, 45r, 45tl, 47br, 48/49c, 50c, 52cr, 53tc, 54tl, 55br, 55tr, 55tl, 55rc, 58bl, 58/59c, 59tr, 65br, 66bl, 68tl, 69cr, 72cl, 73tr, 73bl, 75cr, 77cr, 78tl, 81tr, 82l & 82cl, 82/83cb, 83tr, 84tl, 84cl, 84br, 86/87c, 90l, 90bl, 91tr, 91cr, 91br, 92tl, 93ct, 94l & 94bl, 94/95c, 106br, 113tc, 116tl, 118br, 120tl. P.I.X; 109t. Planet Earth Pictures; OFC (c, 2nd from right), 1, 3cr, 3tr, 3tl, 3cl, 5br, 9br, 10bl, 11br, 11tl, 13rc, 13tl, 14/15t, 15br, 15tr, 16tl, 17b, 17tr, 18b, 18t, 20br, 20tl, 20tr, 21bl, 23cl, 23c, 23r, 24tl, 24/25t, 26tl, 28/29r, 30/31c, 31br, 31tr, 32br, 34bl, 35c, 37cl, 43tl, 43tr, 44/45c, 46t, 46b, 47tr, 47rc, 48tl, 50/51b, 51cl, 51tl, 51tr, 53b, 54/55c, 54/55b, 57tl, 64cl, 66l & 66cl, 66/67c, 67cr, 67br, 68bl, 69tr, 70/71 (main pic), 70/71cb, 70/71ct, 72l, 72cr, 72/73c, 73cr, 74tl, 74bl, 74/75c, 74/75cb, 75br, 76bl, 76br, 76/77c, 77t, 77cl, 79tr, 79br, 80tl, 81c, 81tl, 82/83ct, 83br, 85b, 86tr, 86b, 87b, 87tr, 88tl, 88/89ct, 89tr, 89c, 90/91, 92bl, 94/95cb, 95cr, 96l & 96bl, 97/98b, 97tr, 97t, 98/99t, 98/99c, 98/99b, 99br, 100br, 100c, 100tr, 101bl, 102tl, 102tr, 102c, 102br, 103t, 103c, 103cr, 104l, 104tl, 105c, 105b, 108/109b, 109br, 110tl, 110bl, 111c, 111b, 112tl, 112bl, 113tr, 114bl, 114cr, 115tl, 115c, 115tr, 116c, 116cl, 116/117ct, 117tr, 117cl, 117br, 118/119c, 118bl, 119tr, 119br, 120l & 120bl, 120/121t, 121t, 122tl, 122bl, 123br, 124tl, 124bl, 124/125c, 125tl. SATC, Australian Tourist Commission; 32tl. Spectrum Colour Library; 32c, 34/35cb. Still Pictures; 7br, 30bl, 33r, 34c, 34tl. Survival Anglia; 46c. Telegraph Colour Library; 11tr, 70tl, 78bl, 78/79c, 82/83c. Tony Stone; 92/93 (main pic), 123cl. Every effort has been made to trace the copyright holders and we apologize in advance for any unintentional ommissions.

We would be pleased to insert the appropriate acknowledgement in any subsequent edition of this publication.

UNDER THE OCEAN

The oceans cover nearly three-quarters of the Earth's surface, so it's not surprising that they are home to many lifeforms. Tiny fish can be found here as well as the biggest animal to have ever lived on Earth – the blue whale. Even in the darkest, hidden depths of the sea, specially adapted creatures can survive the terrifying conditions found at the bottom of the ocean. On the sea bed, the pressure and weight of the water is tremendous and no sunlight penetrates the watery depths. Only by creating their own light, and by finding ingenious ways to catch their prey, can life survive. Many ocean creatures are also extremely poisonous and deadly, thus ensuring their own survival in this kill-or-be-killed environment.

IN THE RAINFOREST

At least half of all the world's animal and plant species live in rainforests – and this should come as no surprise as the warm, wet atmosphere is ideal for providing plants and animals with all they need to survive. Most rainforests have an annual rainfall of 250 cm (almost 100 inches) which falls constantly throughout the year. Many animals that live in the rainforests have brightly coloured skin to warn others that they are dangerous, making this a beautiful but hazardous place. The forest is also covered by a thick, green canopy which means the forest floor receives little sunlight. Beautiful tropical birds, monkeys and other creatures live in the canopy, trying to keep out of the reach of deadly snakes and jungle cats.

BIRDS OF THE DESERT

Many different species of birds are found in deserts. In the deserts of North America, birds such as the cactus wren live in nest-holes or branches of the spiny, tree-like cactuses that grow there. The thorn-studded plants give protection from snakes and other predators that might eat the young birds in the nest.

THE SUN-SCORCHED EARTH

Many of the deserts of the world are large. Together they cover over a quarter of the Earth's land surface. This is the Namib Desert, which covers one-third of Namibia and stretches 1,290 km (800 miles) along the coast of southwestern Africa. It receives less than 1.3 cm (0.5 inches) of rainfall a year.

ARMOUR-PLATED

Scorpions are particularly abundant in desert regions. They hide by day and hunt by night, using their powerful pincers to crush the insects and spiders on which they prey. Their long tails end with a sting, which they use to defend themselves.

HOPPING AROUND

Like many desert animals, this little hopping mouse avoids the searing heat of the day. It emerges from its burrow after dark when it is cooler and safer to hop about looking for food. Desert mice and rats are extremely important to life in the desert, as they are prey to a wide number of the larger animals, including owls, snakes and foxes.

THE HOSPITABLE DESERT

t is midday. Directly overhead the Sun burns fiercely in a cloudless sky. The glare is so strong that without sunglasses it makes your eyes hurt. The parched ground stretches out all around you. In the distance the rocks shimmer from the intense heat. All is silent. Nothing moves. The desert is lifeless. Or is it? At first sight, the sun-baked land of the desert is a barren place unable to support any kind of animal or plant life whatsoever. But, in fact, most deserts have an abundance of life – the animals are simply avoiding the hottest time of the day. Wait until the Sun is lower in the sky and the heat has lessened, and you will see the desert begin to stir. So even though you would find the desert a hellish place to live, it is home to many animals and plants, specially adapted to the harsh conditions.

DESERTS OF THE WORLD

This map shows the desert regions of the world (shaded yellow). Most have a very hot climate, but a few that lie outside of the tropics are cool. Both arid and semi-arid regions have low rainfall. The arid regions have an annual rainfall of less than 25 cm (10 inches), and often much less. Semi-arid regions receive between 25 and 50 cm (10-20 inches).

TROPIC OF CANCER

EQUATOR

TROPIC OF CAPRICORN

LIVING IN THE DESERT

This woman is from the Tuareg tribe, a group of people from Africa's vast Sahara Desert. They are nomads, moving from place to place looking for grazing grounds for their herds. The Tuaregs keep sheep and goats, and use camels to carry water and provide milk. Most humans cannot live easily in the desert conditions, yet desert tribes have adapted to the hardships and prospered. Over many centuries they have learned how to use the land, plants and animals to survive.

7

WEATHER & CLIMATE

COLD DESERTS

Some deserts are among the coldest places on Earth. In extreme Arctic areas (above) it is the cold, rather than the heat and lack of moisture, that makes it difficult for life to survive. Water is locked up in snow and ice. In tundra regions, vast treeless zones of the far north where the subsoil is permanently frozen, there is a brief summer when some of the snow melts, and plants and animals can get the water they need to flourish and reproduce.

Deserts are places where no one knows for certain when it will rain next. Months and even years may pass between rainfalls. And in some desert areas, such as in the Atacama Desert of South America, it may never rain at all. This lack of rain contributes to the dryness of the deserts, which is often made worse by the hot, dry winds that blow over them. In the daytime, the ground temperature can soar to over 80°C (176°F). In these conditions, a light shower of rain from passing clouds instantly evaporates before it touches the ground, and the precious rainfall is lost. As the Sun sets, the temperature drops sharply because there are no clouds to stop the heat from escaping into the sky. As a result, it is not unusual for deserts to be frosty at night. Thus deserts have the biggest temperature ranges in any one day.

UNDER A CLOUDLESS SKY

From space, the Atacama Desert of South America can be clearly seen. This desert is sandwiched between the Andes, the mountain chain that runs down the entire west coast of the continent, and the Pacific Ocean. The Andes act as a barrier to rain-bearing clouds blown across from the west. In addition, the effect of the Humboldt Current, a cold sea current that flows along the coastal edge of South America, is to dry the sea air before it reaches the land. This desert is one of the driest regions in the world.

PACIFIC OCEAN   THE ANDES

ATACAMA DESERT

DUST DEVIL

A miniature whirlwind whips up dust and sand into the air. Dust and sand storms are common whenever the wind blows strongly over the open desert. A storm blowing sand over 3,000 metres (9,800 ft) high can suddenly appear on the horizon and engulf everything almost without warning. The dust or sand is so thick that not even the glaring desert Sun can be seen through it.

DESERT SAND

The great, constantly shifting dunes are formed by the wind, making it virtually impossible for any desert plant to take root and grow. Sandy deserts are not as common as other types – deserts covered by rocks and stones make up three-quarters of the world's deserts. These sand dunes in Namibia are among the tallest in the world, reaching heights of 370 metres (1,200 ft).

FLASH FLOOD

Rainfall can happen very suddenly in some desert regions. Sometimes the rain is so torrential that it may last for hours, even days. The massive amounts of water cover the land, cascade over rocks and fill deep ravines. Often they gouge out deep channels as they move, carrying tonnes of sand and rocks with them. Flash floods usually occur in the mountain regions of deserts. The water may travel many kilometres from the site of the rainfall.

GHOST TOWN

This abandoned building is in the once-thriving diamond mining town of Kolmanskop, in Namibia. Although the desert sand has all but swallowed up the town, buildings and items, such as machinery, cars, beds and tables, are likely to remain intact for hundreds of years. This is because the desert has a preserving effect. The lack of moisture means that wood, leather, fibre and other natural materials do not perish or rot away, and metal does not rust and crumble into dust. Thus, deserts have a long memory – the abandoned signs of human activity scar the environment for many generations unless or until they are removed.

DESERTS OF THE WORLD

Deserts are found across the world, but most are found in belts between the Tropics of Cancer and Capricorn, in areas where the strong Sun and hot wind bring little rain. The Sahara and Kalahari Deserts of Africa are of this type. Deserts are also found in the shelter of mountain ranges, such as the North American deserts of the Great Basin and Mojave. They are called rainshadow deserts because as the moist winds cross the mountains, they lose their moisture in the form of rain. By the time the winds reach the plains beyond the mountain peaks, there is little or no moisture left. The desert of central Australia and the Gobi Desert of Asia exist because they are too far from the sea – the rain-carrying winds simply never reach them.

DESERT HOMES

This thatched granary stands in a village in the Thar Desert of India. The villagers have learned how to make the best use of any rainfall. One way is to build walls around their fields, so that the rain water will not rush over the land and erode the soil. The walls trap the water, allowing it to soak into the ground and feed the plants.

NORTH AMERICA

KEY
1 Arabian Desert
2 Atacama Desert
3 Gobi Desert
4 Great Basin
5 Great Sandy Desert
6 Great Victoria Desert
7 Kalahari Desert
8 Mojave Desert
9 Namib Desert
10 Sahara Desert
11 Simpson Desert
12 Sonoran Desert
13 Thar Desert

SOUTH AMERICA

MONUMENT VALLEY

This spectacular desert area on the Arizona-Utah border in the USA is a rock desert which was formed by erosion over millions of years. The cliff-like rock formations, called buttes, which are hundreds of metres high, are made from sandstone. The rock is worn away by the wind and, occasionally, water. The valley floor itself is bare and flat, and is strewn with the broken fragments and fine particles of the rock slabs of fallen buttes.

DESERTS LONG AGO

These beautiful rock paintings show that the Sahara region was once a less arid place, able to support those animals that are found today on the great grassy plains of the African savanna. The drawings were made around 5,000 years ago, when the climate of North Africa was much wetter. As the climate changed and the weather became hotter, the lakes and water holes slowly began to dry out, creating the desert we know today.

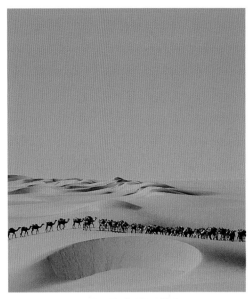

THE SAHARA DESERT

The Sahara Desert in North Africa is the largest desert in the world. It covers almost a third of the African continent, and is almost the size of the United States. The great camel caravans seen on the Sahara are usually controlled by the Tuaregs, who traditionally travelled across vast areas of the desert, even up to the Mediterranean, to trade. But not all of the Sahara is sand. The sandy regions, called ergs, only make up one-fifth of the area – the rest is made up of mountains, stony plateaus and dust-filled basins.

THE SIMPSON DESERT

The Simpson Desert is a region of about 145,000 sq km (56,000 sq miles) in central Australia. Here sand dunes up to 35 metres (115 ft) high and 450 metres (1,500 ft) apart run parallel across the desert. In between these sand-dune crests grows spinifex grass, which is specially adapted to the dry desert conditions. The Simpson Desert is home to some of the most unique desert animals, such as marsupial mice, but these have become threatened since the introduction of the cat to Australia.

DESERT PLANTS

Plants have evolved special ways of living in the desert. Only the shifting sand dunes are plant free, as it is impossible for the plants to establish themselves. But elsewhere, plants are able to exist, and have adapted in a variety of ways. They have to survive long periods of drought. The rain, when it comes, is unpredictable – it could be a light shower or it could fall in torrents. Many plants deal with these extremes by using every drop of moisture they can take up in their roots, storing it in their stems or in underground tubers (fleshy roots).

ANNUAL PLANTS

In the desert, some plants, such as this yellowtop, avoid the problem of the drought by remaining as seeds. When it rains, the seeds suddenly sprout and the plant grows very quickly, taking advantage of the moisture in the soil before it dries up. The plant flowers and then produces seeds ready for the next time it rains. After seeding, the plant dies.

Englemann's prickly pear

CACTUS FLOWERS

Cactuses produce some of the most beautiful and colourful flowers in the desert. Some cactuses have only one flower at a time, while others have many. The flowers only last for a short time – from a single night in some cases to several days in others.

Claw cactus

GIANT SAGUARO CACTUS

These giant tree-like plants of the North American deserts can reach a height of 16 metres (52 ft) and a weight of 10 tonnes.

They send out a network of shallow roots up to 10 metres (33 ft) in all directions. The roots are strong and dense to both absorb as much water as possible and keep the plant upright in strong winds. These majestic cactuses take a very long time to grow – this one may be over 200 years old.

Cactuses suck up water when it rains and hoard it in their stems, using it gradually to grow during the long periods of drought. When there is another downpour, they can refill their tanks

Leaves have been reduced to spines, to minimize water loss and to protect the plant

Stem has a waxy surface to stop water loss

Ribs or pleats expand when it rains to store water in its sponge-like cells

Roots spread out near the surface to take up rain water

TUNISIAN OASIS

Oases are natural springs fed by water that comes from a distant source, such as rain-fed mountains, maybe hundreds of kilometres away. The water flows underground through the rock until the rock comes to the surface. Desert people settle by oases as the surrounding area is very fertile. There, plants and trees flourish, such as these palms, which are harvested for dates. In Australia, oases are called billabongs.

CREOSOTE BUSH

This bush, so named because of its odour, flourishes when there is lots of space around it. It spreads its roots and absorbs the moisture that has collected a few centimetres below the surface of the soil. It gleans the water so effectively that no other plants can grow within several metres of it. The waxy coating on the leaves helps to reduce water loss.

DESERT OAKS

These trees in the Simpson Desert of Australia send down long roots, called tap roots, deep in the soil in search of water. A network of roots at every level ensures that the trees capture every drop of moisture that is in the soil. Plants that grow on valley floors often use this method to absorb water. Tap roots may grow tens of metres in order to reach an underground water supply.

WELWITSCHIA

This unusual-looking plant grows in the Namib Desert. The Namib borders the coast and at night a fog often rolls in from the sea, leaving drops of moisture on the ground and on the plants. The Welwitschia has a fat, swollen root, from which grow long, strap-like leaves that can absorb water droplets. Any water that is not taken up runs off the leaves to be collected by the plant's roots.

DAYTIME CREATURES

I n the desert, the Sun beats down on the exposed land for most of the day. There are no clouds to absorb the sunlight and the sparse vegetation gives little shade. By midday, the soil and rocks are unbearably hot to touch, so it is not surprising that desert animals seek shade during the hottest part of the day. Nothing moves unless absolutely necessary. So daytime creatures are at their most active when the Sun is not so hot – in the morning and late afternoon – when there is less danger of their bodies over-heating.

BIRD OF PREY

By staying well above the baking ground and the layer of hot air above it, the buzzard is less affected by the intense heat. Flying also creates a stream of air across its feathers, which helps to cool its body. Birds can also find high places on which to perch – perhaps a tall cactus – which are not as hot as the ground below. In addition, from their lofty vantage points, buzzards and other birds of prey can easily spot a lizard or bird that would make a good meal.

DESERT LOCUST

Locusts are large grasshoppers. They have a skeleton on the outside of the body, called an exoskeleton, which is covered in a waterproof layer of wax to prevent water loss. They get all the water they need from the plants they eat. They fly in vast swarms, sometimes in their billions, devouring crops and natural vegetation as they do so.

FERAL CAMELS

In the 19th century, one-humped camels of Arabia, called dromedaries, were brought into Australia to help people explore the desert. Now they can be found roaming free, spending the day grazing on grasses and scrub. The two-humped bactrian camels of the Gobi desert still roam wild.

TIGER SWALLOWTAIL

The beautiful tiger swallowtail butterfly feeds from a flower. These insects get their moisture from nectar, the sweet-tasting liquid found at the base of many flowers. Butterflies use their long tongues to suck up the nectar, and as they move around the flower their bodies pick up pollen. When the butterfly visits a similar type of flower, some of the pollen is transferred and the flower is pollinated, and can now produce seeds.

GILA MONSTER

This lizard of the American west begins its hunt when the Sun rises above the horizon. At first it moves about sluggishly and then, as its body warms up, it becomes more and more active as it looks for food – insects, lizard eggs, young birds and small desert mice. However, as the Sun starts to become unbearable it needs to find shade. The gila monster is the largest North American lizard, growing to 60 cm (2 ft) and its bite is poisonous – its Mexican relative is the only other poisonous lizard.

TARANTULA

This Mexican red-kneed tarantula lives in the deserts of Mexico and the southern USA. It hides in its silk-lined nest for most of the day and then emerges in the afternoon, using its long, hairy legs to run down its prey, which are mainly beetles and other insects. It uses poisoned fangs to kill its food and protect itself from attack.

WHAT A LARK!

Of all the desert creatures, birds are the ones that cope with the intense heat most easily. Their feathers are good insulators. When it is cold the feathers keep the bird warm. But feathers are also good at keeping the heat out. This makes it possible for birds to sit in the desert sun without over-heating. When birds get too hot, they reduce their temperature by fluttering their throats. This desert lark is active throughout most of the day.

NIGHT-TIME CREATURES

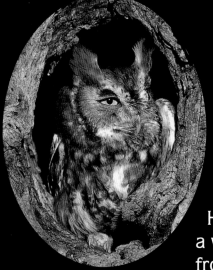

EASTERN SCREECH OWL

Like most owls, this bird is nocturnal. It is a bird of prey – it hunts other animals for food – and stays comfortable in its nest-hole during the day, conserving its energy. But as night falls, it leaves its home to search for the mice, insects and lizards that become active after dark. The screech owl is well adapted to hunting at night. Extremely good eyesight and very sensitive hearing enable it to locate its prey. Its feathers help it to stay warm in the cold hours of darkness.

As darkness falls, the temperature begins to drop. Cold-blooded creatures (animals unable to make heat to warm their bodies, such as lizards) loose their warmth quickly and so must retire to their burrows when it gets too cold. However, for most desert creatures the coolness is a welcome relief from the stifling heat, and they stir from their day-time slumber as the Sun begins to set. For them the hours of darkness are the best time to be active. Small mammals, such as desert mice, move about timidly looking for seeds and bits of dead vegetation to eat. By dawn, the ground and rocks will have lost nearly all the stored heat from the previous day. This is the coldest time of the day, and many of the nocturnal animals return to their holes and crevices. Soon the day-shift creatures will be on the move, often led by the birds, which are the desert's early risers.

NIGHT-TIME TRACKS

Sometimes the only evidence of night-time creatures is their tracks in the sand.

FENNEC FOX **SIDEWINDER SNAKE** **KANGAROO RAT**

KANGAROO RAT

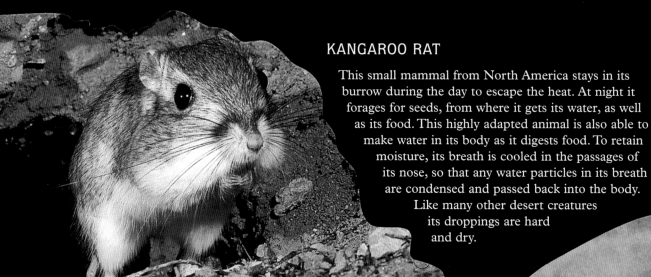

This small mammal from North America stays in its burrow during the day to escape the heat. At night it forages for seeds, from where it gets its water, as well as its food. This highly adapted animal is also able to make water in its body as it digests food. To retain moisture, its breath is cooled in the passages of its nose, so that any water particles in its breath are condensed and passed back into the body. Like many other desert creatures its droppings are hard and dry.

NIGHT-HUNTING GECKO

Although most lizards are daytime hunters, not all lizards retire to their crevices as soon as the Sun goes down – as long as the earth and rocks still retain some warmth, they are able to continue to hunt for food. This gecko is from the deserts of central Asia. It grows to 20 cm (8 inches) in length, and lives in a burrow.

HOTSON'S FIVE-TOED JERBOA

The jerboa can be found in the Sahara Desert. It has short, weak forelimbs, long hind limbs and a long tail, making it look like a small kangaroo. It ventures out of its nest as soon as night falls, in the hope that the darkness will give it some protection from fennec foxes and other enemies. As the jerboa hops about, it looks for seeds, tufts of grass and other bits and pieces of plants that make up its diet. Some of its food may have blown into its area by the wind.

FENNEC FOX

These hunters of the Sahara Desert have large triangular ears for picking up the sounds made by gerbils and other small animals as they scamper around the desert looking for food. Fennec foxes move silently, their noses to the ground, sniffing for a scent trail that may lead to a tasty meal. Its large eyes help it to see in the darkness of the night.

FINDING WATER

Water is essential for life – it replaces lost fluids and is vital for many body processes. So how are desert creatures able to survive the hot, dry conditions that can last for months, or even years, before there is even a drop of rain? The answer is that they have all found ways of conserving water. A few of them do not even need to drink. They either get what little water they need from their food or they make it in their bodies as part of the process of turning food into body fuel. Birds have the advantage of being able to fly to a source of water. Other animals make long journeys to find the water they need.

A WATER CARRIER

Sand grouse build their nests up to 40 km (25 miles) from a pool. When the eggs hatch, the males ferry water back to their chicks in their feathers. As they paddle in the pool, their breast feathers become wet, and when they are fully saturated they fly back to the nest where the chicks 'suck' the water off with their beaks.

WATER FROM PLANTS

Like some other large desert animals, the dorcas gazelle of Africa finds much of the water it needs from the plants it eats. The leaves contain the plants' sap, and this watery fluid is enough for the gazelle to survive.

AT THE WATER HOLE

The red kangaroo, one of the largest of the kangaroo family, is found all over Australia, including the desert regions. It gets very little water from the grasses it eats, and so the kangaroo makes a trip from its grazing grounds to a water hole every day. Red kangaroos live in herds, or mobs, of around 10 to 15 animals.

CATCHING WATER

This beetle from the Namib Desert takes advantage of the fog that often hangs over the desert at night. It climbs to the top of a sand dune and stands facing the sea with its head downwards and its body lifted up into the air. As water droplets form on its body, they roll down into the beetle's mouth.

FRUIT JUICE

The fruits of plants are a good source of water. These are the fruit of the prickly pear, which are moist and juicy. Birds, beetles and other creatures that eat these fruits have little need of drinking water.

OPEN WIDE

The road runner is a bird often seen running across the deserts of North America on its slender legs. The adult bird feeds its chicks by dropping food – a lizard or snake – into the chick's gaping mouth, and in doing so trickles water from its beak into the throat of the chick, allowing it to drink.

BODY FLUIDS

The desert jackal hunts animals for food, and the kill provides it with enough water so that it does not need to make special trips to a water hole. The water is in the form of body fluids, which it swallows as it feeds. For example, blood is a body fluid, and about half of it is made up of a substance called plasma, which is mainly water.

SURVIVING THE HEAT

The best way of surviving the heat is simply to avoid it. So the majority of desert animals rest in the daytime in a cool burrow or crevice in the rocks. Those that do not go underground find shade to wait out the heat, though this can be difficult in deserts where vegetation is sparse with few leaves to cast large shadows. Even the slightest movement of a leg or the head produces heat in an animal's body, so at the hottest time of the day most animals keep as still as possible. Even lizards and snakes, which need warmth in order to be active, are at the mercy of the hot conditions. Their bodies would dangerously over-heat if they stayed out in the open.

COOLING DOWN

The emu is a large flightless bird that lives in most parts of Australia, including the desert areas. They cope with the heat of the desert quite well, and when they need to cool themselves, they flutter their throats to lose heat.

WATER RETENTION

Some species of toad survive well in the desert dryness. They store up to half their body weight of water in their bladder. Desert toads are able to survive an extremely long drought in this way.

SUN SHADE

This ground squirrel is active during the daytime, taking its portable 'parasol' with it wherever it goes. For when it gets too hot, it erects its bushy tail over its head and spreads the hairs so that it casts as wide a shadow as possible. It cocks its tail to adjust the position of the shadow so that it always falls on its body.

GOING UNDERGROUND

This African lizard (below) is perfectly adapted to the harsh conditions found in desert dunes. It is called a sand swimmer from the way it appears to swim through the sand with fish-like movements of its body. The surface of the dune gets unbearably hot in the daytime, but just a few centimetres below the surface it is much cooler. The grains of sand are so smooth and dry that the lizard is able to swim through the sand to where a beetle is moving around on the surface. It then pops out to seize the beetle in its strong jaws.

WATERTIGHT SKIN

This horned viper's watertight skin allows it to retain all the water in its body.

COOL EARS

The huge ears of the North American jack rabbit act like radiators to give off heat. A fine network of blood vessels running just under the skin cool down the rabbit's body, as air blows over its ears.

Fringes on its feet allow it run on the surface of the dune

Small legs which it holds close to its body when 'swimming' through the sand

Heavy tail is an aid to 'swimming'

Tight-fitting scales and stream-lined shape for travelling quickly through the sand

Skin does not sweat so water is conserved

Sharp, chisel-shaped nose for pushing the sand aside as it travels forwards

Sunken ears for smooth shape

WHEN IT RAINS

FAIRY SHRIMP

Swarms of tiny fairy shrimp swim in muddy pools left by a cloudburst. They appear so fast that it is as if they had fallen with the rain. In fact, they have hatched from eggs that have been in the soil or blown on the wind since the last rain – which in some instances may be as long as 50 years ago. They are in a hurry to grow and mate before the puddles dry out and they die. By the time all the water has gone, their eggs have been laid ready for the next generation of these tiny creatures.

For most of the year, the desert looks barren and it is a wonder that animals and plants exist there at all. Often the richness of life is a surprise, and only really becomes apparent when it rains. This is the trigger that brings the parched, dry earth to life, for there are many creatures and plants that cram all the active parts of their life cycle into one short period when water is abundant. Until the downpour, they remain dormant and unseen, but afterwards they flourish, reaching maturity with incredible speed before the puddles and lakes dry up in the unrelenting Sun. Then when all the water has evaporated and the land is once again dry and parched, all that is left is their shrivelled remains. But they have fulfilled their purpose – to reproduce and ensure there are future generations of life.

SPADEFOOT TOAD

The gift of water is too much to miss for the spadefoot toad, for this is the signal for the toad to emerge from the soil, where it buries itself, to mate in the pools of water. Once the eggs are laid and fertilized, the toads hop away to feed. They must build up their reserves before they again burrow into the ground to wait for the next fall of rain. In the meantime, the eggs develop very fast. Within a day or two the pool is swarming with tadpoles which must finish their development before the pool dries out. Only a few will mature into toads and make their home in the desert.

BLOOMING DUNE

After a shower of rain the desert can become a riot of colour. On the right, evening primrose plants are flowering in the shifting sand of the Sonoran Desert in the USA.

DEVIL'S CLAW SEED POD

This weird 'growth' is a devil's claw seed pod. In the desert, seed heads and seed pods quickly become brown and dry, and dead looking. But as soon as there is a cloudburst, they appear to come to life, for the rainwater causes the parts to split allowing the seeds to fall to the ground and grow.

ALGAE

The dust that blows around the desert contains microscopic spores – cells that are so small that they can only be seen under a microscope. In the pools these develop into the filaments of simple plants called algae. The algae grow fast and reproduce not by mating, but by shedding more microscopic spores into the water. When the pool dries up, the algae dies. However, the spores have a tough skin and are able to withstand the hot desert conditions. They blow about the desert until the next fall of rain.

BEFORE AND AFTER

The semi-arid region of Namaqualand in South Africa is shown here before and after the rain. The picture on the right shows the dry parched landscape. The picture on the left shows the desert after the rain, when dormant seeds have suddenly burst into life.

FOOD CHAIN

HAWK

$\downarrow$

LIZARD

$\downarrow$

BEETLE

Large birds of prey, such as the hawk, prey on smaller animals, including lizards and rodents. These feed on the many beetles and insects which live in the desert.

FROM PREDATOR TO PREY

This desert cat has caught a sand viper, a poisonous snake. The snake was probably on the look out for its own prey, perhaps a mouse, when it was caught. Carnivores are often food for other meat eaters.

PREDATORS & PREY

For almost any animal, the desert is a dangerous place, not only because of the heat and lack of moisture, but also because many creatures are the prey of larger animals. The most intense feeding activity occurs when the heat of the day has passed – in the late afternoon and into the evening. This is when many creatures come out of their burrows or nest holes to find food. Fortunately for both daytime and night-time feeders most deserts have an abundance of invertebrates, such as spiders, ants and beetles, which is the staple food for many birds, rodents and reptiles. In turn, these become prey for the larger meat-eating predators. In the desert, most predators have adapted themselves in ingenious ways to the harsh desert conditions.

LOOKING FOR BUGS

The pointed face and spines of the desert hedgehog of North Africa are very similar to hedgehogs found in European countries. However, their ears are larger. This helps them to catch every sound in the desert. Their large ears also help them to lose heat. The desert hedgehog is always on the search for beetles and other insects on its nightly forages.

SAHARAN CHEETAH

A desert cheetah in West Africa runs down its prey. It can reach a speed of 96 km/h (60 mph), but only over a short distance, after which it will usually give up if it has not caught its prey. Top predators like cheetahs also provide food for scavengers like vultures and hyenas.

FENNEC FOX

DESERT MOUSE

SEEDS

A THORNY DEVIL

This weird-looking creature from Australia gets its name from the thorn-like spikes that cover its body. Also called the moloch lizard, its method of feeding is to sit by a trail of ants and flick them up into its mouth using its tongue. It can eat several thousand ants at any one time. Since the ants are eaten one by one, the meal can take quite some time!

Foxes pounce on mice as they scurry around the desert looking for seeds and other plant food. Plants make their food through photosynthesis. In this way, it is the energy of the Sun that begins the desert food chain.

A DEADLY HUG

A kingsnake of North America grasps the head of a mouse while it uses its body to squeeze its prey to death. Kingsnakes are so-called because they kill and eat other snakes, including the venomous rattlesnake, one of the most feared creatures of the desert. The kingsnake is immune to the venom of other snakes, and so its victims have been known to try and beat off their attacker with their body rather than defend themselves by biting.

COMING UP FOR A MEAL

The golden mole is a dune-living predator, tunnelling energetically through the sand and coming above ground to catch insects, like this locust.

DEFENCE

D esert animals are in a constant battle to stay alive. Part of the battle is to escape from their predators when attacked, and so they have evolved an amazing number of ways to avoid their enemies. Some of these are very simple, such as running or hopping away at high speed when threatened. The jack rabbit, for example, can reach 70 km/h (43 mph) in a series of long springing bounds when chased by a hungry coyote. Other defences, such as camouflage, when animals simply blend into the scenery, may be less athletic but can be equally effective.

GOING UNDERGROUND

Ground squirrels found in North America and Africa build extensive networks of tunnels in which they live. In North America, they make a very loud warning 'chirp' when a bird of prey soars into view before bolting for cover.
If a rattlesnake comes near, they make more warning chirps and 'flag' their tails to indicate the position of the snake.

SPEED

Many animals simply flee from their attackers as fast as they can. A large predator, such as a desert fox or cat, will approach its prey by stealth, so that it can get close enough to leap. But once spotted, the prey will try to get away, with the predator giving chase. If the animal is fast enough, it will out run its attacker and so escape.

PROTECTIVE SHELLS

Tortoises do not need speed to escape their enemies. Their defence is the armoured shell they carry around with them into which they retreat when danger threatens. They withdraw their heads completely, protecting the entrances at the front and back with their scaly skin. This allows them to feed on wild flowers and other plants at their leisure.

CAMOUFLAGE

Most desert animals have a basic colour pattern that suits their habitat, making them blend in with the background. But the chameleon has the added advantage of being able to vary its colour, thus enhancing its camouflage to escape its enemies.

BRIGHT COLOURS

In the animal world, brightly-coloured markings are a warning to other animals that a creature is nasty to eat or poisonous. The colours are designed to make them as obvious as possible. In the case of the coral snakes of North America, the bands of colour are saying, 'Keep away because I've got a poisonous bite!' As a result, most predators stay well clear of the snake and avoid attacking it.

JUST BLUFFING

Sheer bluff is the means by which this Australian frill-necked lizard repels attackers. The large photograph shows the enormous neck frill, which is the main feature of the bluff. Above is the frill fully erected. At the same time, the lizard will also stand on its hind legs and, with its mouth wide open, bob its head and lash its tail back and forth to frighten off its predator.

NESTS, EGGS & YOUNG

Reptiles, such as lizards and snakes, generally lay their eggs and then leave. After hatching, the young must look after themselves. Amphibians, such as frogs and toads, generally make poor parents, too. After the eggs are laid in a pool of water, the adults move on. However, other animals show some form of caring for their young. Social insects, such as ants and termites that live in colonies, have workers that tend and feed the larvae until they become adult. But it is the birds and mammals that make the most effort in raising a family. Their offspring are kept clean, fed and protected until they are old enough to fend for themselves.

RED TAIL HAWKS

These majestic daytime hunters of the North American deserts make their ragged nests high in the prickly branches of saguaro cactuses. This helps to ensure that the eggs and chicks will not get dangerously hot in the unbearable heat of the day. The nest is built out of the reach of predators. At night, the warmth from the parents' bodies stops the chicks getting too cold as the temperature plummets.

MEERKATS

The meerkat, or suricate, of the desert country of southern Africa lives in community burrows. The young are born underground, but as they grow they begin to venture out as a group, and always in the company of adult meerkats. The adults keep a constant lookout for predators, and at the slightest sign of danger they give an alarm and everyone dives for the safety of the burrow.

FENNEC FOX & HER BABIES

Mammals, like this fennec fox, take excellent care of their babies. The female fox suckles her young with milk from a gland called a mammary gland. But first the mother builds an underground nest called a den, where the young will be safe from desert predators. After the babies are born, she feeds, cleans and keeps them warm. As the babies grow, the mother gradually changes the diet from milk to solid food, bringing them desert mice to eat.

DESERT LOCUST

Like a lot of other insects, these mini-beasts show only a basic form of care for their young. The female uses her egg-laying organ, or ovipositor, to drill into the soil before laying her eggs. By placing them underground she hides them from hungry enemies.

HITCHING A RIDE

Scorpions are fearsome hunters but they make excellent parents. After hatching from the eggs, the young scorpions hitch a ride on their mother's back. There they are safe, protected by the mother's strong pincers and deadly sting, until they are large enough to look after themselves.

LIVING TOGETHER

Some desert animals spend their entire lives living together. In the case of insect societies, many thousands of individuals live in a colony, working together to carry out many different tasks, such as nest building, breeding and defence against enemy attack. The degree of organization of these large communities seems incredible, as they function almost like a single creature. Because of this, they are sometimes called 'super organisms'.

SAFETY IN NUMBERS

A flock of ring-neck doves gather at a desert water hole to drink. There is safety in numbers for the doves, for while some of the birds are drinking, the other ones are on the lookout for enemies. This makes it very difficult for any predator to pounce on the flock by surprise.

Other animals that live in groups may not have the same numbers or degree of organization, but they still depend on one another for survival.

NIGHT-TIME PARTNERS

A cactobastis moth sits on a prickly pear cactus. Instead of closing their flowers at night, some desert plants do just the opposite and open them to attract the night-time insect visitors that pollinate them. In return the insects get a rewarding meal of nectar.

GEMSBOK

Herds of this stocky animal are found in the arid areas south of the Sahara Desert. The gemsbok is a type of oryx, and is well adapted to living in the desert. It feeds on dry vegetation, and can go for long periods without drinking. Its cousins once lived in large numbers in the deserts of the Sahara, and the Sinai and Arabian Peninsulas, but they were hunted to extinction. More recently, the oryx was bred in zoos and reintroduced to the wild in the 1980s.

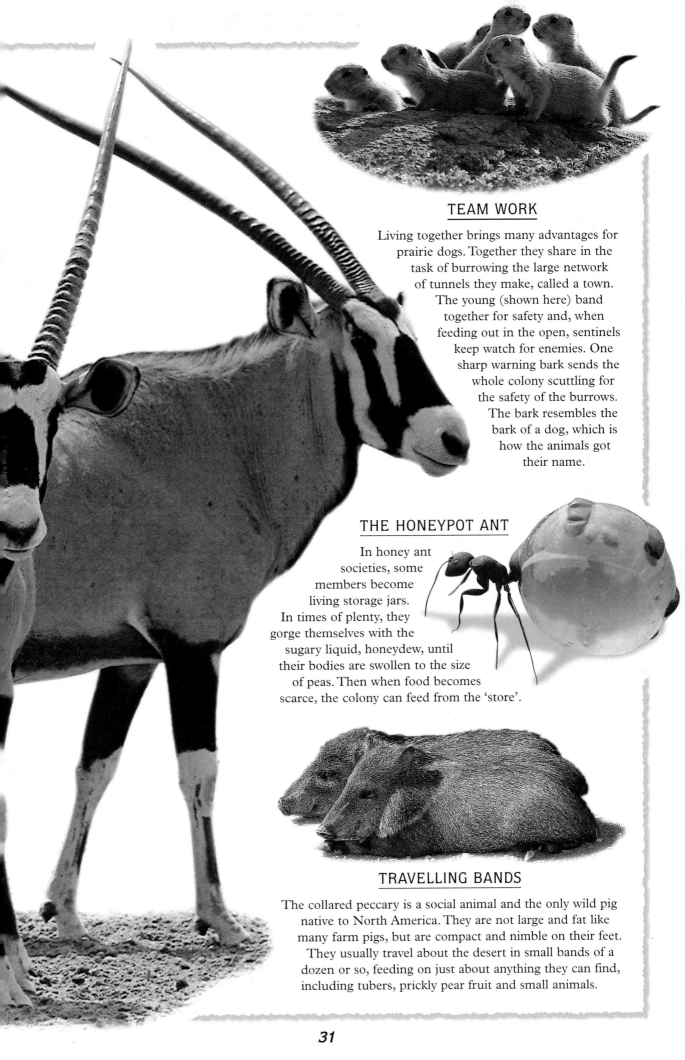

TEAM WORK

Living together brings many advantages for prairie dogs. Together they share in the task of burrowing the large network of tunnels they make, called a town. The young (shown here) band together for safety and, when feeding out in the open, sentinels keep watch for enemies. One sharp warning bark sends the whole colony scuttling for the safety of the burrows. The bark resembles the bark of a dog, which is how the animals got their name.

THE HONEYPOT ANT

In honey ant societies, some members become living storage jars. In times of plenty, they gorge themselves with the sugary liquid, honeydew, until their bodies are swollen to the size of peas. Then when food becomes scarce, the colony can feed from the 'store'.

TRAVELLING BANDS

The collared peccary is a social animal and the only wild pig native to North America. They are not large and fat like many farm pigs, but are compact and nimble on their feet. They usually travel about the desert in small bands of a dozen or so, feeding on just about anything they can find, including tubers, prickly pear fruit and small animals.

PEOPLE OF THE DESERT

espite the harshness of the weather conditions, people who live in the desert are able to make use of what it has to offer to support their families and make a living. For example, in North America, native American tribes, such as the Hopi and Navajo, learned long ago to use the plants and animals of the desert for food, clothing and shelter. And in Africa, the bushmen of the Kalahari Desert know many secrets of the desert, including which plants have tubers that store enough water to provide a drink. Without such special knowledge, people would not survive long in the harsh desert conditions.

LIVING UNDERGROUND

The Australian town of Coober Pedy is on the edge of the virtually waterless Great Victoria Desert. Most of the world's opals are mined here. Its name means 'white man's hole', which refers to the practice of early miners who built their homes underground to escape the high temperatures.

PORTABLE HOMES

The nomads of the Gobi Desert of Central Asia move from one area to another in order to find enough grass for their large flocks of animals to feed on. Their homes, called yurts, can be put up, taken down and transported very easily. The Gobi Desert is one of the largest deserts in the world, about 1,600 km (1,000 miles) long and 1,000 km (625 miles) wide.

AUSTRALIAN ABORIGINES

The Aborigines of the Australian desert are able to supply all their needs from the land. For example, they know which different areas, whether rocky hills or sand dunes, provide the particular species of plants they require or animals to hunt. They know where the water holes are, and they reach the water in dry creek beds by digging away the sand until water seeps into the hole.

FRUITS OF THE DESERT

People living close to oases are able to irrigate the land and produce crops. Often palm trees are grown for their harvest of dates, which may be spread out on the ground to dry in the Sun.

NOMADS OF THE SAHARA

Even the great dune deserts of the Sahara are inhabited by the Tuareg, a nomadic people who lead caravans of camels with goods to trade. They carry cloth, dates, precious metals and other goods to sell or exchange at ancient trading cities for the things they need, such as salt. The nomads wear long flowing cloaks and cover their faces to protect them from the Sun.

LOCAL MATERIALS

A Moroccan basket-maker displays his wares. The people of desert regions have learnt to live in harmony with their environment, taking only what they need in order to survive. By using local resources wisely for producing items for sale or for building materials, they put little demand on the desert.

REFORESTATION

Reforestation projects are becoming necessary in the southern Sahara. Whole villages are becoming involved in such projects, as the trees they plant hold the soil together and prevent erosion from the wind and rain. Areas that have been cleared of trees and shrubs are replanted before they become part of the advancing desert.

SALT MINES

Walvis Bay is on the coastal margin of the Namib Desert. Here the sea water slowly evaporates in the hot Sun, leaving behind a layer of sea salt. Saltpans are similar, only they form in desert basins and rely on the evaporation of rainwater for the surface cover of mineral salts. Salt is a valuable item, and in some cases the deposits are intensively mined, with disruption to the desert environment caused by the extraction itself and the transport used to take the salt away.

PROTECTING THE DESERTS

T he deserts are fragile places which can easily be spoilt. For example, some of the world's greatest oilfields are found in desert areas. Although oil brings much-needed resources to the countries that extract it, the building of wells, storage tanks, oil pipelines and roads inevitably has a harmful impact on the environment. Attempts to make the desert bloom, through irrigation schemes, have also had an adverse effect in many deserts. Desert water contains high levels of mineral salts, and these build up in the soil until no plants can grow. If the animals and plants of the desert are to survive, such as the endangered Gila monster lizard of North America, they must be protected from the thoughtless actions of people.

OIL WELLS

An oil well in Kuwait burns out of control after it was set alight by Iraqi forces. Pollution ruined large areas of desert during the Gulf War in early 1991.

OVER-GRAZING

The number of people living permanently along the desert margin has increased in recent years. The people farm the land, cutting down trees for fuel and keeping herds of grazing animals, such as goats. This has put great pressure on the already sparse vegetation, which is not given enough time to recover properly. As a result the edge of the desert slowly advances, reducing the area for farming.

CITIES IN THE DESERT

Many cities have sprung up in desert regions, such as Las Vegas in the Nevada desert in the USA, famous for its luxury hotels and casinos. The inhabitants of desert cities live and work in air-conditioned buildings. The huge supply of water a city demands cannot usually be met locally. So it must be piped in from rivers or reservoirs perhaps hundreds of kilometres away. A good road network encourages more and more people to visit the desert, diminishing the areas that are left unspoilt.

THE SPREADING DESERT

Along the margins of many deserts are zones of semi-desert. These zones are not true desert, but regions where the rainfall is enough for crops to grow. As more people settle in these areas to farm the land, these areas are turning into desert by poor farming techniques. The map shows the risk of desertification in northwest Africa. The problem was made worse by a severe drought from 1969 to 1973. This led to the first ever United Nations conference on desertification in 1977.

SAHARA

SAHEL

KEY
● Severe risk ● Moderate risk

POLE TO POLE

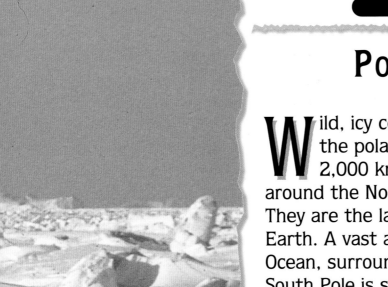

Wild, icy cold and spectacularly beautiful, the polar regions extend for over 2,000 km (1,200 miles) in all directions around the North Pole and the South Pole. They are the last two wilderness areas on Earth. A vast area of frozen ocean, the Arctic Ocean, surrounds the North Pole, while the South Pole is surrounded by a frozen continent called Antarctica. Antarctica is the fifth largest continent and has 90 per cent of all the ice on Earth. Both the Arctic and the Antarctic have long, dark winters when the Sun never shines. During the short, cool summers, the Sun never sets and many animals visit polar lands to feed, nest and raise their young. Only a few especially hardy animals manage to live in the Arctic and Antarctic all year round.

ARCTIC TRAVEL

The harsh terrain and the savage and unpredictable climate combine to make polar travel dangerous and exhausting. In the Arctic, native peoples originally used long, low sleds pulled by husky dogs – bred from Arctic wolves – to transport heavy loads. Huskies are hardy, strong and intelligent and work in a strict hierarchy under the lead dog. It usually takes a year or two to learn how to drive a dog sled. Dog sleds are still one of the best ways to travel in polar regions, but most polar transport is now motorized and includes vehicles such as snowmobiles or skidoos.

FROM POLE TO POLE

The graceful and elegant
Arctic tern flies from
the top of the world
to the bottom and
back again every year – a
round trip of some 40,000 km
(25,000 miles). It flies farther
than any other bird
to spend summer in both the Arctic and
the Antarctic. The Arctic tern probably
experiences more hours of daylight than
any other creature on Earth.

ICY PENGUINS

These penguins are resting on a rare
blue iceberg. About seven species of penguin
live and breed in south polar regions.

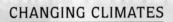

CHANGING CLIMATES

The poles have not always been so cold. Ice has
built up at the poles only during the last 30
million years and the lands around the Arctic
and under the Antarctic ice have been in their
current positions for less than 50 million years.
The continent of Antarctica was probably once
near the Equator where the climate was warmer
and subtropical. Ferns, cycads, trees and other
green plants grew there and dinosaurs roamed
the land. We know little about the prehistoric origins
of the Arctic region but the landmasses have drifted
slowly about and sea levels have changed. This has
sometimes allowed land bridges to form between
continents such as Asia and North America,
along which animals could migrate.

*Dawn redwood
fossils dating
back 100 million
years have been
found in
the Arctic.*

Fierce dinosaurs, such as Allosaurus, once lived in the Antarctic.

NORTH

THE POLES TODAY

The geographic poles are at the
extreme ends of the globe at the
points farthest north and farthest
south in the world. A magnetic pole
lies near each of the geographic
poles, but they are always moving.
Compasses work using a magnetic
needle so they point to magnetic
north and south rather than the
true poles.

SOUTH

WEATHER & CLIMATE

SNOW BLIZZARDS

Strong winds draw heat away from the body and make animals very cold. Sitting curled up with its back to the wind, this husky is trying to expose as little as possible of its body to the freezing wind. Its thick fur helps to keep it warm.

Polar climates are intensely cold and dry, with very strong winds. Cold air moves from the poles towards the Equator, helping to stop the Earth from getting too hot. Antarctica is the coldest and windiest place on Earth, with average winter temperatures of -60 °C (-76 °F) and roaring, ferocious winds of up to 300 km/h (180 mph) producing blizzards and snow drifts. An unprotected person could freeze solid in minutes. Both the Arctic and the Antarctic are cold deserts, since most areas receive less than 240 mm (10 inches) of rain or snow each year. Yet more than nine-tenths of all the world's fresh water is stored in the ice sheets on Antarctica and Greenland. Polar regions have only two seasons, summer and winter. When it is summer in the Arctic, it is winter in the Antarctic, and vice versa. The 24 hours of daylight in summer have led to the nickname 'lands of the midnight Sun', because the Sun is still shining in the sky at midnight.

ARCTIC SUMMER

Caribou (also called reindeer) visit Arctic lands in summer when the top layer of the ground thaws and there are plenty of plants for them to eat. Unfortunately for them, clouds of midges, gnats and mosquitoes also swarm over the marshy ground in summer. The insects are, however, useful food for some of the birds that visit the Arctic for the summer season.

CURTAINS OF LIGHT

Glowing, shimmering curtains of light called auroras sometimes appear in polar skies, especially near the magnetic poles. They happen because the Earth's magnetic poles attract charged particles given off by the Sun. When these particles strike gas particles in the Earth's atmosphere, coloured light is radiated. Auroras are called the *Aurora Borealis*, or Northern Lights, in the Arctic and the *Aurora Australis*, or Southern Lights, in the Antarctic. Auroras are difficult to photograph because they are very faint and move rapidly.

WHY ARE THE POLES COLD?

The Sun's rays bring heat and light to the Earth. But the Earth is curved like a ball, so the Sun's rays are weaker and more spread out at the poles than at the Equator. The rays also have to travel farther through the atmosphere to reach the poles and the atmosphere absorbs much of the heat, making the poles colder. The white ice and snow at the poles reflect back between 50 and 90 per cent of the Sun's heat, making the poles colder still.

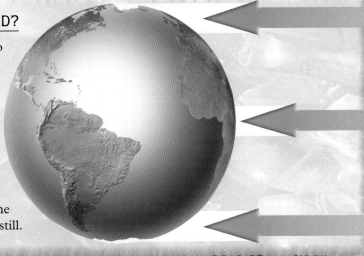

THE NORTH POLE

Although the areas around the North Pole and the South Pole are both cold places and home to many similar animals, they have a very different geography. The North Pole lies in the middle of a shallow, frozen ocean surrounded by the northern edges of Europe, Asia and North America. This whole area is called the Arctic, named after Arktos, the Great Bear star constellation, which dominates the northern polar skies.

THE ARCTIC

The Arctic region consists mainly of the Arctic Ocean, which can be as much as 1,600 km (1,000 miles) across and has a thin skin of ice on top. The largest island in the Arctic Ocean is Greenland, which is covered in a thick ice sheet. Also part of the Arctic is a band of land called the tundra, which means 'treeless land'. This covers the northern parts of Canada, Alaska, Russia and Scandinavia. On maps, an imaginary line called the Arctic Circle surrounds the Arctic area.

CANADA
BERING STRAIT
ARCTIC OCEAN
NORTH POLE
BAFFIN BAY
GREENLAND
ANTARCTIC CIRCLE
ICELAND
NORWEGIAN SEA
GREENLAND
BARENTS SEA
FINLAND
RUSSIA

LIVING IN THE ARCTIC

Polar bears are the only animals to live and hunt on top of the Arctic Ocean – polar bear tracks have even been found near the North Pole itself. There are probably about 20,000 polar bears wandering alone over the remote Arctic ice floes as they hunt for seals beneath the ice.

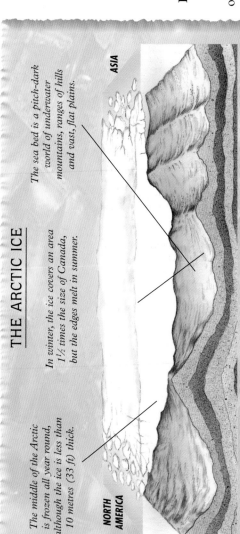

ASIA

THE ARCTIC ICE

In winter, the ice covers an area 1½ times the size of Canada, but the edges melt in summer.

The sea bed is a pitch-dark world of underwater mountains, ranges of hills and vast, flat plains.

The middle of the Arctic is frozen all year round, although the ice is less than 10 metres (33 ft) thick.

NORTH AMERICA

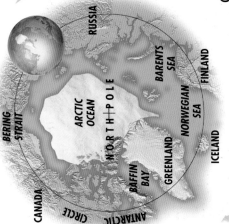

ARCTIC FLOWERS

The tundra landscape is low and flat, with no trees, but many low bushes, lichens, mosses and grasses.

In summer, parts of the tundra burst into bloom as flowering plants rush to flower and produce seeds before the short spell of warm weather ends. There are over 500 species of flowering plants in the Arctic.

THE SOUTH POLE

The South Pole lies in the middle of the continent of Antarctica – the name means 'opposite the Arctic'. Antarctica is a mountainous continent that is almost completely covered by a gigantic ice sheet and is the size of Europe and the USA put together. Unlike the Arctic, the Antarctic has very little ice-free land, even in summer. It has no land mammals, and fewer plants and animals than the Arctic.

SOUTHERN
ANTARCTIC CIRCLE
SOUTH POLE
OCEAN

THE ANTARCTIC

The Antarctic region is separated from the rest of the world by the stormy waters of the Southern Ocean. In winter, ice extends hundreds of kilometres out into the ocean from Antarctic coasts. There are several groups of remote islands near Antarctica (such as South Georgia), but the nearest landmass is the southern tip of South America, which is about 960 km (600 miles) away. On maps, the Antarctic region is bordered by an imaginary line called the Antarctic Circle.

ANTARCTIC ICE

More than half of the surface of Antarctica lies below sea level.

A few mountains, called nunataks, extend their peaks above the ice.

EAST

If the ice was removed, the land would rise about 550 metres (1,800 ft).

The Antarctic continent is almost completely covered by a gigantic ice sheet, up to 4 km (2.5 miles) thick.

WEST

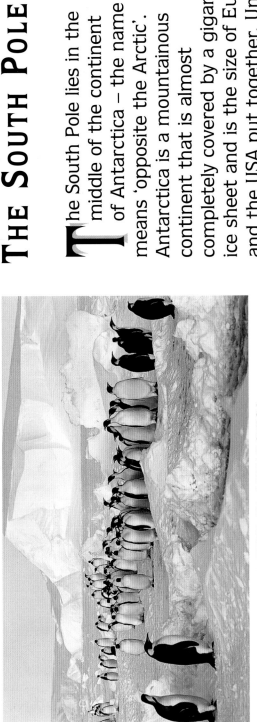

WINTER IN ANTARCTICA

Penguins live only in the southern half of the world, mainly in and around Antarctica, so polar bears and penguins never meet. Only two species of penguin, the Adélie and the emperor, breed on the Antarctic continent itself. Most penguins leap ashore to breed during the summer, but the emperor penguin (as seen here) lays its eggs in the winter. This allows the chicks to hatch in early spring and have the whole summer to grow.

ANTARCTIC FLOWERS

Only two flowering plants grow on Antarctica and neither of them looks much like a flowering plant because they have tiny, drab-coloured flowers. The most common is Antarctic hairgrass (above) and the other is a type of pearlwort called *Colobanthus*.

POLAR PLANTS

It is amazing that any plants survive at all in polar lands because of the short summers, thin soils, searing cold winds and lack of moisture. In the Arctic, the soil is permanently frozen below the surface but the top layer thaws in summer. Water cannot drain away, so the waterlogged summer soil is boggy and marshy with many lakes and ponds. Arctic plants have to cope with these wet soils as well as the cold and dry air. They tend to grow close to the ground in tussocks, cushions, carpets and rosettes to keep out of the wind, to trap moisture and to avoid being crushed by snow and ice. The leaves of polar plants are often thick and waxy with few breathing holes to stop water escaping.

MEAT-EATING PLANTS

Sundews gain extra nutrients by trapping insects on their sticky flypaper leaves. The leaves are covered with special hairs that have drops of sticky glue on the ends. Any insect attracted to the glistening drops is likely to become trapped on the sticky hairs. The leaf then slowly curls around the insect's body and the hairs pour out digestive juices to turn the body into a soupy pulp. The plant absorbs its insect soup and, after a day or so, all that is left of the insect is a dry, empty husk.

ANCIENT LICHENS

In both polar regions, the most successful plants are mosses, lichens and algae. There are over 400 different lichens in the Antarctic, some of which are at least 10,000 years old but still very small because they grow extremely slowly in the cold conditions.

ARCTIC WILLOW IN AUTUMN

Although there are no tall trees on the tundra, the remarkable Arctic willow manages to survive by creeping along the ground. Its branches never rise more than 10 cm (4 inches) from the ground, but may be more than 5 m (16ft) long. Its shoots and leaves contain more vitamin C than an orange.

ARCTIC POPPY

The bowl-shaped flowers of the Arctic poppy work like a reflecting dish to focus the Sun's rays onto the central part of the flower. The flower also turns to follow the path of the Sun. Both these adaptations help to keep the seeds warm so they will develop quickly – before the summer Sun disappears from the sky. Arctic poppies grow in low cushions, like many polar plants.

POLLINATION

The hairy 'fur' on a bumblebee helps it to keep warm but few insects can survive in these cold places. Most Arctic plants cannot rely on insects to carry their pollen. Instead it is spread by strong winds from plant to plant so that seeds can grow. Many plants reproduce by growing new pieces of themselves, such as small bulbs or creeping stems called runners.

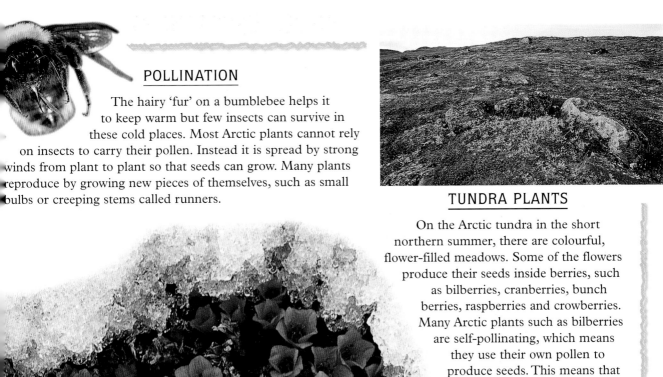

TUNDRA PLANTS

On the Arctic tundra in the short northern summer, there are colourful, flower-filled meadows. Some of the flowers produce their seeds inside berries, such as bilberries, cranberries, bunch berries, raspberries and crowberries. Many Arctic plants such as bilberries are self-pollinating, which means they use their own pollen to produce seeds. This means that they do not have to rely on the wind, or insects, to spread the pollen. The new plants, which grow from the seeds, are identical to their parent plants.

FROM FLOWER TO SEED

Since the Arctic summer is so short, plants such as this purple saxifrage must produce their seeds and ripen them in one season. The seeds must be ready to sprout or germinate as soon as possible the following summer. They spend the winter resting in the soil, waiting for the warmth and moisture they need to trigger germination.

PLANT EATERS

The leaves, shoots, roots and berries of tundra plants provide food for a variety of animals, including this brown bear. Bears eat as much as possible in the summer to build up stores of fat which will last them through the winter. There is even a berry called a bearberry.

ARCTIC ANIMALS

From tiny, buzzing insects and scurrying lemmings to huge caribou, polar bears, whales and walruses, the Arctic and tundra lands are full of a surprising variety of animals, both in the sea and on the land. Many mammals and birds are migrants, moving north in summer from the lands or seas outside the Arctic Circle. These include caribou (reindeer), ducks, geese, swans, wading birds and some seals, which visit the Arctic to feed and breed. This means that the number and variety of Arctic animals change dramatically with the seasons. The few hardy Arctic residents include musk oxen, polar bears, some seals and whales, Arctic foxes, and birds such as the ptarmigan and ivory gull. Unlike the Antarctic, there are land birds as well as sea birds. Summer lakes and bogs provide breeding grounds for millions of mosquitoes and other biting flies, while flowering plants on the tundra attract butterflies, bees and beetles.

SEALS

The most numerous and widespread seal resident in the Arctic is the ringed seal, which may even appear at the North Pole. The other main Arctic seals, the harp seal (above) and the hooded seal, are migrants. Some harp seals travel about 3,500 km (2,000 miles) to give birth on Arctic ice floes in late winter. By the time the seal pups are old enough to hunt on their own, summer has arrived and there are plenty of fish in the sea.

THE ARCTIC FRITILLARY BUTTERFLY

The Arctic fritillary is one of the few butterflies found within the Arctic Circle and is one of only about six species of butterfly to survive in Greenland. Its dark markings help to absorb warmth from the Sun and the speckled pattern on its wings camouflage it from enemies, such as birds and spiders.

WALRUSES

Living only in the Arctic, walruses are not seals, but are closely related to them.

Both male and female walruses have two long, sharp, curved tusks, which are actually upper canine teeth. In fights, walruses attack each other with their tusks. Walruses use their fleshy noses and whiskers to find clams and other shellfish, crabs and worms on the sea bed.

LEMMINGS

Tunnelling among Arctic plants, rocks or soils are large numbers of lemmings. These small rodents are plant-eaters, which form an important source of food for meat-eating animals, such as Arctic foxes, stoats and owls. Lemmings make ball-shaped nests out of plant material and females often give birth to the first litter of the year beneath the snow at the end of winter. If there is plenty of food, one female can have as many as 84 young in one year.

THE LITTLE AUK

There are no penguins in the Arctic but little auks, or dovekies, look rather like them. They have come to look similar because they have adapted to a similar environment. Both birds have a streamlined shape for swimming underwater and flipper-like wings. The main difference is that the little auk can fly, but penguins cannot. The little auk is not much bigger than a thrush but it is very successful at living in the Arctic.

WILD WOLVES

Although wolves live in a variety of habitats, they are well adapted to life in the Arctic. Their thick fur keeps them warm and often turns white for camouflage. This helps them to get close to their prey without being seen. Arctic wolves hunt in packs so they are able to catch large animals such as caribou and young musk oxen. They will also eat carrion and small mammals, such as voles, lemmings and hares. Superb hearing and a keen sense of smell allow a pack of wolves to track down its prey. The wolves relentlessly pursue their quarry for long distances without tiring thanks to their strong bodies and long legs.

LIFE IN SLOW MOTION

The cold temperature of the water and the scarcity of available food mean that life runs in slow motion and animals without backbones tend to grow slowly. They live longer and reach larger sizes than species from warmer places.

The sea bed around Antarctica is sometimes covered with countless red starfish, some of which can live for nearly 40 years.

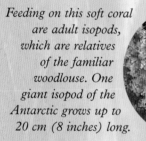

Sea spiders walk or crawl about on the ocean floor on their 10 or 12 long legs. They either suck the juices from soft-bodied animals or browse on hydroids and moss animals.

Feeding on this soft coral are adult isopods, which are relatives of the familiar woodlouse. One giant isopod of the Antarctic grows up to 20 cm (8 inches) long.

ANTARCTIC ANIMALS

There are few ice-free areas of land on the continent of Antarctica and the largest animal that lives on land all year round is a tiny wingless midge only 12 mm (0.5 inches) long. During the summer, however, the ice around the fringes of the continent melts and animals, such as penguins, seals and sea birds, come ashore to breed. On the islands around the Antarctic continent, the climate is less harsh and the greater variety of plant life encourages a greater variety of animal life, particularly birds such as albatrosses and petrels. Sheathbills are the only land birds to live all year round in Antarctica; other birds leave in the winter. Although life on the land is restricted by the ice and the climate, life in the seas around Antarctica is incredibly rich – twice as rich as in the Arctic. Small animals include plankton, corals, anemones, sponges, worms and starfish, and there are also larger creatures such as fish, seals and whales.

BLUE WHALE

The Southern Ocean around Antarctica has a greater variety and quantity of whales than any other ocean. They range from toothed whales, such as killer whales, to baleen whales, such as this blue whale. Baleen whales filter food through fringes of tough skin (called baleen) that hang down inside their mouths. Blue whales are the largest animals that have ever lived. Adults weigh more than 30 elephants and are longer than a jumbo jet.

BLUE-EYED SHAGS

The feathers of the blue-eyed shag soak up water so its weight increases and it can sink and dive after fish in the ocean. But after a swim, the bird has to spread out its wings to dry. Shags never fish far from their nest or roost sites and they use their rookeries all year round. Their rookeries are on remote Antarctic islands and the very northern tip of the Antarctic peninsula.

MINIBEASTS

The dominant land animals in Antarctica are tiny minibeasts called mites and springtails (right). Mites are related to spiders while springtails are wingless insects. Both have antifreeze in their bodies to stop them freezing to death. They reproduce whenever the temperature rises above freezing.

WEDDELL SEAL

Weddell seals spend the whole winter under the ice that covers the seas around Antarctica. They make breathing holes in the ice with their teeth and may have to grind through ice many metres thick. If they fail to keep their breathing holes open, the seals will drown. These hardy seals can dive to depths of about 580 m (1,900 ft) and stay underwater for up to 70 minutes. They communicate using a series of weird calls that bounce off the ice and carry for many kilometres underwater.

ADÉLIE PENGUINS

Adélie penguins spend the winter out at sea. When they return to their breeding colonies on the Antarctic continent in October, there is still a lot of sea ice between them and their nest sites. They have no time to wait for the ice to melt, so they march inland over the ice for distances of up to 100 km (62 miles).

SURVIVING THE COLD

Animals living in both polar regions have similar adaptations to help them survive in these hostile environments. Thick layers of fur, feathers or fatty blubber help to keep out the cold and trap the heat given off by the body of a bird or a mammal. Many are forced to migrate to warmer places in the winter but a few small mammals (such as the Arctic ground squirrel) hibernate over the winter. Ice fish and some minibeasts survive all year round thanks to the antifreeze in their blood. The dark colours of minibeasts absorb the Sun's heat and help them to keep warm.

BLUBBER

The thick blubber of this baby seal stops body heat escaping. Blubber is a thick layer of fat under the skin. It can be up to 25 cm (10 inches) thick. Whales also rely on their blubber for warmth.

Cubs stay with their mother for a year or more to learn how to survive and hunt on their own.

Hairs in the coat are hollow and trap warm air near the body, like double glazing.

Under the fur, a thick layer of blubber insulates the bear against the cold and acts as a food store when food is hard to find.

Polar bear hairs are transparent, allowing the Sun's heat to penetrate through the fur to the skin, which is black and absorbs the heat.

BODY WARMTH

When emperor penguin chicks are about eight weeks old, they are too big to hide under their parents for warmth. Instead they huddle together and rely on their dense, fluffy feathers and the warm bodies of their fellow chicks to keep warm. Conditions are so hard in the Antarctic that only 19 per cent of emperor penguin chicks will survive their first year.

ANTIFREEZE

The antifreeze in the blood of ice fish stops ice crystals forming. In the middle of winter, when the top of the ocean is solid ice, these fish manage to survive in the almost frozen waters below. Fish without this adaptation would freeze to death in these conditions.

SHELTER

Wandering albatross chicks sit on the nest for up to a year through winter blizzards and snowstorms. They are protected from the cold by thick down feathers and an insulating layer of fat under the skin. The chick's survival depends on how successful its parents are at finding food in the stormy Southern Ocean.

Small round ears lose little heat.

POLAR BEARS

The polar bear of the Arctic is the largest bear in the world – an adult male can be nearly twice as tall as a person and six times as heavy. Its bulk helps it to keep warm, as does its thick fur coat which is made up of two layers, a thick underfur of short hairs, and an outer coat of long guard hairs. These hairs stick together when they get wet, forming a waterproof barrier.

A polar bear's nose is just about the only part of the body that is not furry.

Its big paws have rough, furry, non-slip soles to grip slippery snow and ice.

Yellow-white fur is useful for camouflage. The colour of the fur comes from the way the light reflects off the colourless, hollow hairs.

Powerful legs enable a polar bear to walk and swim long distances when hunting prey, although it becomes overheated after running for a long period of time.

ANIMALS ON THE MOVE

Walking and running over slippery ice and soft snow is not easy. Polar mammals and birds often have wide, flat feet with fur or feathers between the toes. This spreads out their weight like human snowshoes and stops them sinking into the snow. On slippery slopes, some penguins lie down on the snow and slide down like living toboggans. Polar birds that can fly need powerful wings to survive the strong winds and make long migration journeys. They need plenty of food to give them the energy to fly. Before migrating, they store energy in the form of fat in their bodies, as do the many polar animals who migrate to and from the Arctic and Antarctic every year. The blubber of whales, seals and penguins is a useful source of energy for their long journeys. It also helps to smooth out their body shape, making them more streamlined so they can swim faster and farther.

PORPOISING PENGUINS

In order to breathe while swimming fast, penguins often leap out of the water. They travel through the air at speeds of up to 25 km/h (16 mph). This technique of leaping in and out of the water is called porpoising. Under the water, penguins use their stiff wings to almost fly through the water. They steer with their feet and tails.

MIGRATION JOURNEYS

Caribou, or reindeer, are always on the move, trekking incredible distances of up to 9,000 km (5,600 miles) – the longest journeys of any land mammal on Earth. They move between forests on the edge of the Arctic, where they shelter in the winter, and the Arctic tundra, where they feed in summer. The caribou follow well-marked trails that are often hundreds of years old and usually cross many fast-flowing rivers. A line of migrating caribou may stretch for 300 km (190 miles).

JET SET

Torpedo-shaped squid are an ideal shape for shooting through the water fast. They use a method of jet propulsion to accelerate rapidly. By pushing a narrow jet of water out of a funnel at the front end of the body, the squid shoots off in the other direction, which is backwards. The funnel can be curved for swimming forwards. Larger squid can swim at up to 30 km/h (19 mph), very useful if they are escaping from predators such as sperm whales.

WIDE WINGS

The spectacular wandering albatross has the largest wingspan of any bird. It spends most of its life at sea gliding on its huge wings. The long, narrow shape of the wings is ideal for picking up the air currents and it glides at great speed for long distances, hardly beating its wings at all. It can reach speeds of 88 km/h (55 mph) and keep going for days at a time.

WHALE TAILS

The flat, rigid tail flukes of a whale move up and down to push it forwards through the water. Swimming movements are powered by large muscles lying above and below the backbone. About a third of a whale's body is pure muscle. The huge bulk of a whale's body is supported by the water pushing up against its skin. Its blubber also helps it to float more easily.

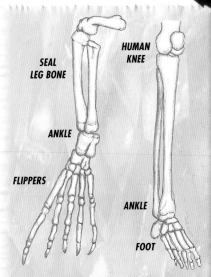

SEAL
LEG BONE

HUMAN
KNEE

ANKLE

FLIPPERS

ANKLE

FOOT

SEAL FLIPPERS

From the outside, the flipper of a seal looks very different from a human arm or foot. But inside, the bones are the same. As seals have evolved over millions of years, their limbs have become webbed paddles, which push them through the water faster than our hands and feet. The flipper has a bigger surface without gaps and pushes more water out of the way at each stroke. True seals use their back flippers for swimming; sea lions and fur seals use their front flippers instead.

SNOWSHOE FEET

Arctic hares have wide, flat feet with lots of fur underneath. This helps them to run or walk over snow without sinking in very far. Their long back legs allow them to bound along quickly, which is vitally important when they are escaping from predators such as Arctic foxes.

LAND FOOD CHAIN

ARCTIC FOX

ARCTIC HARE

LEAVES & BERRIES

Land food chains are very different in the Arctic and Antarctic. The Arctic has a lot of land plants for plant-eaters such as Arctic hares, which in turn are prey to meat-eaters like Arctic foxes. The Antarctic has very few plants. A typical food chain might be a plant-eating mite feeding on fungi and being eaten in turn by a meat-eating mite.

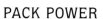

PACK POWER

Hunting in packs of up to 20 animals, gray wolves range over large areas to find enough food to eat. They can run for many hours, tiring out their prey. Many packs follow migrating herds of caribou, picking off old, young and sick animals that stray from the main herd. The wolves disable their prey by biting its legs and hindquarters, then kill with a bite to the throat.

PREDATORS & PREY

In polar oceans, predators and their prey are remarkably similar in both the Arctic and the Antarctic. Killer whales are top predators in both polar regions. They attack in groups, like wolves on dry land, which allows them to catch and kill bigger animals than they could on their own. Predators are usually strong, fierce animals, with sharp teeth, claws or beaks to help them catch their prey. They often have to move very fast to catch up with their next meal before it escapes. Food is scarce in polar regions and predators may go without food for five days or more.

PATIENT HUNTER

To catch a ringed seal, a polar bear waits patiently for a seal to come up for air. Its white coat makes it blend into the white, snowy background as it keeps still and silent for up to four hours. As soon as the seal comes to the surface, the polar bear pounces, killing the seal with a blow from its huge paws and a bite at the back of the skull. The bear is so powerful, it can drag a seal out of the water through a small hole in the ice several metres thick.

SEA CATS

Like their spotted namesakes on land, leopard seals are strong, swift, solitary hunters. They hide in the water near penguin colonies, making surprise attacks on penguin chicks learning to swim. Chicks make easy prey because they are not very good at diving, so have little chance of escape. The leopard seal often plays with its victim for 10 minutes or more. Then it beats the dead penguin chicks against the surface of the water, stripping their feathers off and turning the skin inside out to get at the flesh. Leopard seals also eat other seals, squid, fish and krill.

FIERCE AND FURRY

The wolverine is strong for its size and has a powerful, crushing bite. Its large feet allow it to chase after its prey up to a distance of 65 km (40 miles) before it needs a rest. Once it has made a kill, a wolverine quickly takes the body of its victims to pieces, hiding most of the meat to eat later, when food may be hard to find.

SOUTHERN STINKERS

Giant petrels are nicknamed 'stinkers' after their unpleasant smell. They are about the size of a vulture and use their powerful hooked beaks to kill penguins, shags and squid, as well as to tear the meat from seal carcasses.

ARCTIC PREDATORS

There are more predatory birds in the Arctic than the Antarctic because of the variety of small mammals on tundra lands. Snowy owls, like this one, feed mainly on lemmings, swooping down to catch them in their strong, curved talons.

OCEAN FOOD CHAIN

KILLER WHALE

SEAL

SQUID

KRILL

PLANT PLANKTON

In polar waters, killer whales are top predators feeding on seals and penguins. Sea birds and squid prey on fish and tiny animals and plants, called plankton, that float in the water.

SLIPPERY MOUTHFUL

Puffins have special spines on the tongue and top part of the bill. These help them to catch and hold slippery fish, such as sand eels, and carry them back for their chicks. One puffin can hold up to 60 small fish at a time. Puffins catch their food by diving and chasing their fishy prey underwater.

DEFENCE

SEA BIRD COLONIES

By nesting in large colonies on steep, rocky cliffs, sea birds make it very difficult for predators to reach their chicks and eggs. Birds will dive-bomb predators that get too close and shriek alarm calls to their fellow nesters. Birds that nest in cliff-top burrows, such as puffins, are also well hidden from the eyes of their enemies.

Penguins zooming through the water, caribou galloping across the tundra, snow geese flying up out of reach of Arctic foxes...one of the best means of defence is to move as fast as possible. There is also safety in numbers. Herds of mammals, flocks of birds and shoals of fish help each other to spot danger and may co-operate to drive predators away. Nesting in remote and inaccessible places, such as remote Antarctic islands or steep sea cliffs, also reduces the chances of being attacked. Some prey animals try to avoid being seen by having camouflaged fur or feathers that match their surroundings. But not all prey animals are cowards; some have formidable weapons, such as horns or tusks, and are prepared to stand and fight for their survival.

HEAD TO HEAD

Although this polar bear has the advantage of sheer size, the walrus has its tusks to use as weapons against such predators. Its very thick, leathery skin is also useful against the polar bear's sharp teeth and claws. Walruses are fiercely protective of their young, which could be the reason for this stand-off.

COLOUR CHANGE

Many Arctic animals have different coats in different seasons. In winter, the ptarmigan is white so it is hard to see against a snowy landscape. In summer, when the snow has melted, it grows brown feathers to blend in with rocks, soil and plants.

BRAVE LEMMINGS

In the winter, lemmings are hidden from some of their predators in their tunnels under the snow, although Arctic foxes seem to be able to find them easily and ermine, or stoats, are slim enough to chase lemmings through the tunnels. If lemmings are cornered, they put up a hostile defence. Their brightly patterned fur may serve to warn predators of their aggressive behaviour and unpleasant taste.

DANGEROUS NOSE

To warn off enemies or intimidate rivals, male hooded seals can inflate an extraordinary structure on their nose. This 'hood' is an enlargement of the nose cavity and can be inflated to form a vast sac about twice the size of a football. As well as the hood, male hooded seals can also force the lining of one nostril out through the other nostril to form a red balloon. When the seal shakes the balloon from side to side, it makes a loud 'pinging' noise.

HORN CIRCLE

Musk oxen are the size of ponies and are big and strong enough to have only two real predators – wolves and humans. Their horns are long, curved and sharply pointed with a solid horny band across the forehead. Males use their horns to fight for females but they are also useful for defence. A herd of musk oxen will form a tight circle, with their sharp horns facing outwards and calves or weaker animals sheltering in the middle. This strategy works well against wolves but is not very successful against people with guns.

COURTSHIP

At the start of the brief summer breeding season, many birds and mammals go through elaborate displays and ritual fights to make sure they find and keep the right partners for mating. Rival males, such as caribou, walruses and elephant seals fight each other for the right to mate with a group of females. Animals such as musk oxen and wolverines mark their territories with special smelly messages designed to keep out rival males or attract females. Pairs of Antarctic skuas use their long, loud calls for the same purpose. Courtship displays are usually loud and noisy affairs. They may take a great deal of effort and use up lots of energy.

FENCING UNICORNS

The long tusk of the male narwhal, a type of Arctic whale, may have given rise to the legend of the unicorn. Tusks were sold in many countries long before people had seen the animal. Only male narwhals have a tusk and they may use them to fight other males. Males are sometimes seen 'fencing' with their tusks on the surface of the sea.

At the same time, they make the courting animals very obvious to passing predators. But they are necessary to allow females to find the strongest and fittest males and to test whether the partners are ready and able to mate and care for young.

ELEPHANT SEALS

Male elephant seals are up to 10 times heavier than females and have a huge, swollen nose similar to an elephant's trunk. In the breeding season, the strongest males guard a group of females for mating. They fight rival males and roar challenges to them through their extraordinary nose, which acts like a loudspeaker. The oldest and biggest males usually win the fights. Males do not eat during the breeding season since they are constantly on guard on the breeding beaches. The beachmasters cannot afford to leave their females to catch food in the sea because another male will sneak in and take their place.

PENGUIN RITUALS

The striking golden-yellow neck and ear patches of the king penguin are used to attract a partner during courtship. Like other seabirds they need to display together to reinforce the pair bonds between partners before they can mate together.

CARIBOU

Male, or bull, caribou use their antlers during the autumn rut, or mating season. They have contests where they clash their antlers together or have neck-wrestling matches with their antlers locked together. These contests decide which of the bulls are strongest and best able to gather, and keep, a small group of cows safe from challenges by other bulls. After the rutting season, the bulls shed their antlers and grow new antlers for the next breeding season.

WANDERING ALBATROSSES

These magnificent birds live for over 80 years and tend to stick with one partner for life. When pairs are forming or newly formed, they take part in a long courtship display, but established pairs do not need much courtship. During the display, the male attracts a female by pointing his beak upwards, holding out his wings and whistling. When a female arrives, the two birds dance face to face. They make a variety of noises, clap their bills together loudly and fence with their huge, hooked bills. When they have paired up, the birds sit side by side on the nest area, nibbling each other's necks and calling softly.

A pair of king penguins display their brightly coloured necks.

Crested penguins swing their heads in a wide arc.

Adélie penguins bow during pair-bonding.

King penguins have a special 'advertising' call.

NESTS, EGGS & YOUNG

Most polar animals lay their eggs or give birth to their young in the brief summer. In fact, many animals only visit these regions for breeding. They choose to come to these hostile places because there is plenty of food in summer, as well as more space and fewer predators than in warmer places. Two exceptions to the summer breeding cycle are emperor penguins and polar bears, which both rear their young through the winter months. The richest food in polar regions is in the sea and many parents have to take it in turns to look after the young while their partner goes off to feed. Sometimes they may leave the young on their own or gathered in crèches.

POLAR BEARS

Polar bear cubs stay with their mother for at least a year while she teaches them to hunt and survive in the Arctic. For the first few months she feeds the cubs on her rich milk, which is about 30 per cent fat. At birth, the cubs are helpless and tiny – only about a thousandth of their mother's weight. They are well protected from the weather and predators inside a warm snow den, dug by their mother. While she is in the den, the mother polar bear cannot feed and lives off fat stored in her body.

FEATHER NEST

The female eider duck plucks soft down feathers from her own breast and uses them to line her nest. These fluffy feathers trap warm air and help to keep the eggs warm so they develop properly. If the parent birds have to leave the nest, they pull the down feathers over the nest like a warm duvet. Eider ducks nest on small, remote islands in the Arctic Ocean but their eggs and young are still in danger from predators; such as gulls and foxes, as well as the weather.

SNOWY OWLS

When there is plenty of food, such as mice, voles and lemmings, snowy owls may raise seven or eight chicks in one year. If food is scarce, they may not nest at all. The nest is a shallow scrape on the ground, lined with moss or feathers. Owls do not lay all their eggs at once, so there may be chicks of different sizes in the nest. If there is not enough food to go round, the largest owlet will eat the smallest and then the next smallest, and so on. This rather cruel behaviour ensures that at least one youngster has a chance of surviving.

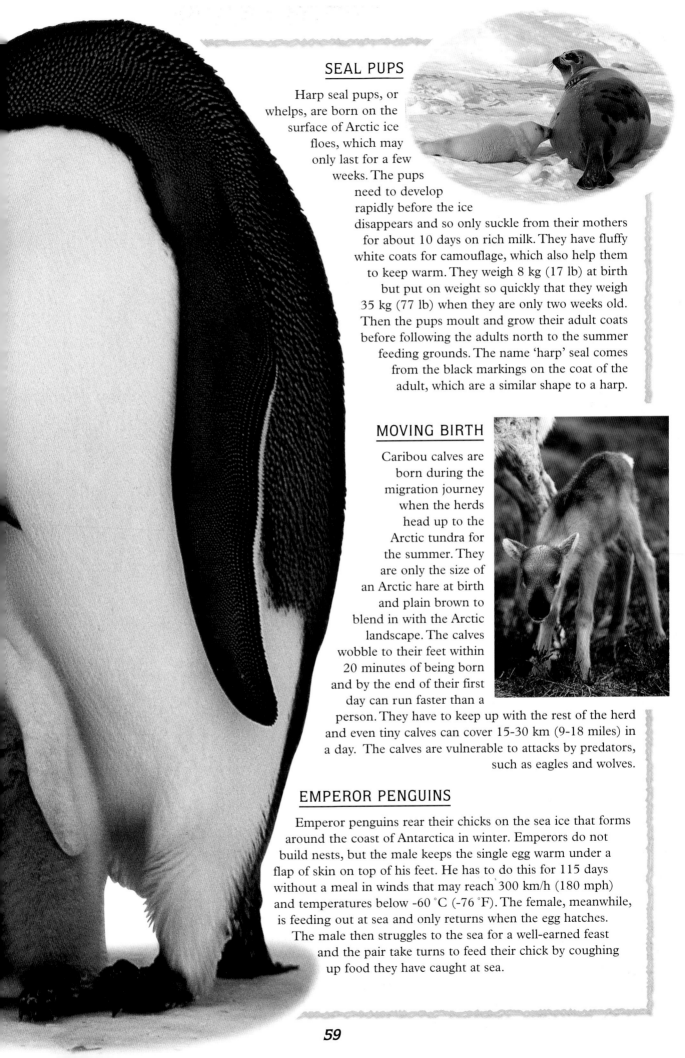

SEAL PUPS

Harp seal pups, or whelps, are born on the surface of Arctic ice floes, which may only last for a few weeks. The pups need to develop rapidly before the ice disappears and so only suckle from their mothers for about 10 days on rich milk. They have fluffy white coats for camouflage, which also help them to keep warm. They weigh 8 kg (17 lb) at birth but put on weight so quickly that they weigh 35 kg (77 lb) when they are only two weeks old. Then the pups moult and grow their adult coats before following the adults north to the summer feeding grounds. The name 'harp' seal comes from the black markings on the coat of the adult, which are a similar shape to a harp.

MOVING BIRTH

Caribou calves are born during the migration journey when the herds head up to the Arctic tundra for the summer. They are only the size of an Arctic hare at birth and plain brown to blend in with the Arctic landscape. The calves wobble to their feet within 20 minutes of being born and by the end of their first day can run faster than a person. They have to keep up with the rest of the herd and even tiny calves can cover 15-30 km (9-18 miles) in a day. The calves are vulnerable to attacks by predators, such as eagles and wolves.

EMPEROR PENGUINS

Emperor penguins rear their chicks on the sea ice that forms around the coast of Antarctica in winter. Emperors do not build nests, but the male keeps the single egg warm under a flap of skin on top of his feet. He has to do this for 115 days without a meal in winds that may reach 300 km/h (180 mph) and temperatures below -60 °C (-76 °F). The female, meanwhile, is feeding out at sea and only returns when the egg hatches. The male then struggles to the sea for a well-earned feast and the pair take turns to feed their chick by coughing up food they have caught at sea.

LIVING TOGETHER

Living in groups mainly for the breeding season is common in many polar animals such as sea birds, penguins and some seals. But other polar animals live in groups with an organized social structure all year round, sometimes with a leader that keeps them all together. In these groups, the young stay with their mothers or both parents for a year or more, learning how to survive. Usually only the female young stay in the group and the males leave to mate with females outside their own family. Relationships between the individuals in a group can become quite complex, with some animals becoming more important than others and each animal having its own place in the group. Group living has many advantages, from helping each other to find food and stopping other animals from stealing food, to banding together to fight predators and protect the young.

KILLER WHALES

Hunting in groups called pods, killer whales co-ordinate their movements by constantly making clicking and calling sounds to each other. The pod hunt like a pack of wolves on land. They attack narwhals, beluga whales and seals, sometimes tipping seals off ice floes. Group hunting allows killer whales to overcome very large prey, such as blue whales, the largest animals in the world.

CARIBOU

The largest herd of caribou in the world is probably the George River herd of North America, which is made up of 750,000 animals, but smaller herds may be thousands strong. For most of the year, herds of caribou are made up of females and their young. Mature males usually live separately from the females and sometimes move together in compact bands of between 100 and 1,000 animals. The only time when males and females of all ages come together is during the autumn breeding, or rutting, season. Then the adult males fight to keep a group of between five and forty females for mating. The females move freely between groups held by different males, leaving and joining them when they want to.

WOLVES

The body language of the wolves within a pack shows their status or ranking within the group. A top, or dominant, wolf will stand erect with its ears and tail pointing upwards. It may also show its teeth and growl. A subordinate, or low-ranking, wolf (on the left of the picture) crouches down, turns down its ears and holds its tail between its legs. Instead of growling, it whines to show it recognizes that the other wolf is superior. Every time one wolf meets another, they use their body language to confirm their status in the group. Only the top male and the top female in a wolf pack have cubs. The ranking system within a pack helps the group to survive as they co-operate to catch food and rear young in a hostile environment.

MUSK OXEN

A herd of musk oxen is made up of females and their young, led by one or more strong males, or bulls. In the mating season, younger bulls are driven out of the herd and form all-male bachelor herds, or live on their own. When they grow stronger, they may challenge the master bulls for control of their own herd. In summer, musk oxen live in herds of about 10 animals, but in winter, the herds join up to form groups of 50 or more.

PEOPLE AT THE POLES

ICE SHELTERS

The Inuit igloo, made of a dome of snow blocks, was a temporary shelter, used on hunting trips. Some Inuit still build igloos for this reason today. The inner walls of an igloo are covered in snow, which melts and freezes into a smooth covering of ice. This igloo is lit by a modern pressure lamp, but light and heat were originally provided by oil lamps burning animal blubber. With the addition of body heat, the igloos keep surprisingly warm inside. In winter, the Inuit traditionally lived in houses made of stone and turf and in summer, they moved into skin tents.

For thousands of years, people, such as the Inuit of North America and Greenland, the Sami of Scandinavia and Russia, and the Nenets of Siberia, have lived in the Arctic. Their bodies have become adapted to tolerate the cold and they have developed nomadic, or travelling lifestyles based on hunting wild animals, such as caribou, seals and fish. European explorers, intent on reaching the poles, learned much from the traditional survival skills of these peoples whose tools, clothing and transport were perfectly designed for the harsh polar conditions. Today, the Inuit and other Arctic peoples are abandoning their traditional lifestyles. Most have settled in modern homes, go to the shops for their food and work on modern fishing boats or in mines. In the summer, however, some still go out hunting and fishing, and combine the old and new ways of life.

POLAR TRANSPORT

Modern forms of Arctic transport, such as this motorized toboggan or skidoo, have replaced the traditional dog sledges. They are easier to keep than a team of dogs and their owners can buy fuel and oil instead of having to catch seals to feed to their dogs.

INUIT PEOPLES

Inuit people have many physical features to help them survive in the cold of Arctic lands. They are short and solidly built to help their bodies conserve heat. The thick pads of fat on their cheeks and eyelids help to protect those parts of the body which are exposed to the cold. The heavy eyelids also protect the eyes from the glare of the Sun reflecting off the white snow. Traditional clothing was based on the skins and fur of animals such as caribou, seals and polar bears. This mother is carrying her baby son in a sealskin amaut.

PEOPLE IN THE ANTARCTIC

There are no native inhabitants of the Antarctic and it was only about 200 years ago that explorers first set foot on the Antarctic continent. Today, many people make scientific expeditions to the Antarctic to study the weather, the wildlife, the ice and the rocks. Most of them go there just for a few months in summer, though some stay for the winter. This huge dome protects the buildings of the United States' Amundsen-Scott base at the South Pole.

REINDEER PEOPLE

This Nenet woman, from Siberia, is using her domesticated reindeer to pull a sledge full of her belongings. The reindeer have colourful red and yellow blankets and harnesses. Like the Sami people, the Nenets follow the reindeer herds, eating reindeer meat, milk and cheese and using reindeer skins for making clothes and for trading in other goods. Today, most have settled in permanent villages.

MODERN PEOPLE

Arctic people have endured some of the most difficult living conditions on Earth by making use of animals and materials in their frozen environment. But modern technology has now transformed their lives, allowing them to live more comfortably in a world of centrally-heated homes, motorized transport, synthetic clothing, high-tech weapons, shops and computers. Traditional survival skills are no longer so relevant.

SAMI PEOPLE

The Sami, or Lapp, people of Scandinavia and Russia hunted reindeer from earliest times and used to survive by keeping large herds. They followed the reindeer on their migration, stopping whenever the herd stopped to feed and sometimes helping them across rivers. Some Sami still live in this way today, although the herders' families usually stay in permanent settlements.

PROTECTING THE POLES

The polar regions are important to the survival of the whole Earth. If the polar ice caps melted, less of the Sun's rays would be reflected back into space and the Earth's climate would heat up. If the world's oceans get warmer, they will expand and this, together with all the melted ice, would raise sea levels. Also, the polar plants and animals are part of a big interconnected web of life that maintains life as we know it. If polar wildlife is damaged, it affects other areas too. Environmental problems in polar regions include pollution, damage from mining and drilling, and hunting endangered species. Today, scientific research has shown how fragile the polar lands are and laws have been passed to try to minimize damage and protect these unique and extraordinary regions for the future.

MINING

The trans-Alaska oil pipeline stretches for 1,300 km (807 miles) from the oil fields of Prudhoe Bay to Valdez, where the oil is pumped into supertankers. It was built to minimize damage to the environment, by avoiding important habitats and the nesting sites of rare birds. The pipeline was even raised in some places so that large animals, such as caribou, could migrate underneath. Yet oil spills and damage have occurred.

GLOBAL WARMING

At the moment, the world seems to be getting warmer, causing polar ice melt. This global warming may be due to a build-up of certain gases in the atmosphere. These gases, especially carbon dioxide, trap heat given off by the Earth and stop it escaping into space. This is making the Earth warm up all over the globe. To reduce global warming, pollution and the use of energy need to be cut down so that fewer heat-trapping gases are released into the atmosphere.

HARD TO REACH

The severe weather and difficult terrain of polar regions has helped to protect them from exploitation over the years. But today, with advanced methods of transport and technology, icebreaker ships can even smash their way through to the North Pole. The abundant wildlife and rich mineral resources, such as coal and oil act like a magnet, drawing people towards the poles. Polar resources will become ever more important as those in other parts of the world are depleted.

TOURISM

In the Arctic, tourism is well established and there are wildlife tours and hiking trips. Even in the Antarctic, tourist ships allow their passengers to get really close to sea birds, seals and whales, some of which are very tame (see left). By visiting these beautiful places, people understand the need to protect them. Tourists also bring income and employment to the local people, but they can disturb the habitats and the wildlife they come to see. Their numbers and movements need to be controlled for the sake of the environment.

SCIENTIFIC RESEARCH

Launching weather balloons in the Antarctic is just one of many experiments carried out by scientists to help them understand how the polar regions work. Holes in the ozone layer were first discovered over the Antarctic, and are probably caused by gases called CFCs, which come from such products as refrigerators and aerosols. Ozone holes are larger over the poles because of their special weather conditions. The ozone layer is vital to the planet because it stops most of the Sun's ultraviolet rays from reaching the Earth. Large doses of these rays damage living things.

FUTURE FOOD

Krill are tiny, shrimp-like animals less than 5 cm (2 inches) long, yet they are the most important Antarctic animals. They are food for millions of fish, birds, seals and whales. Since whaling bans were introduced to protect endangered species, fishermen have started to catch krill instead. Krill are almost half protein and are rich in vitamins. The harvesting of krill needs to be carefully monitored to see how it affects other Antarctic animals who depend on the krill for their survival, just as annual meetings are held to decide how much fish and squid can be caught in the Southern Ocean.

UNDER THE OCEAN

Life can be found everywhere in the oceans, from the shallow, sunlit upper waters to the darkest depths. This makes the oceans by far the largest habitat in our world. They cover most of the Earth's surface, yet they are mostly unexplored because of their sheer vastness and power. The frightening sea monsters that the early sailors claimed had attacked their ships on long voyages were certainly flights of fancy. But as you will discover, there are certainly monstrous-looking creatures living in the salty depths. The oceans teem with life. Some sea creatures are tiny. For example, you would need a microscope to see phytoplankton (types of algae that form the basis of all life in the oceans). Others are huge – the blue whale is the largest creature ever to have lived. It grows to over 30 metres (98 ft) and weighs over 150 tonnes. It is now an endangered species due to over-hunting in the past.

NOT JUST A FRIENDLY FACE

The bottlenose dolphin seems to have a knowing smile on its face. It is a very intelligent animal, able to 'talk' to others of its kind with a wide range of grunts, whistles and clicks. Dolphins, like whales, are not fish but mammals, which means they feed their young on milk.

WEIRD & WONDERFUL

The leafy sea dragon is just one of the unlikely-looking creatures of the oceans. It is, in fact, a type of sea horse, which is a small fish. Although it is a poor swimmer, it is well adapted to its life in the beds of seaweed that grow in the shallow waters of Australasia. The festoon of leaf-like flaps along its body act as camouflage, making it hard for a predator to spot it among the weed.

PLANET OCEAN

From space, the Earth is a blue-looking world because of the oceans, which cover nearly three-quarters of its surface. Water is essential for life; it was in the early oceans that life on our planet began. The oceans hide landscapes more varied and spectacular than those found on dry land. There are vast and towering mountain ranges, plunging, gash-like trenches in the ocean bed and wide plains stretching for thousands of square kilometres. Instead of 'Planet Earth', perhaps our world should be called 'Planet Ocean'.

SPEED & POWER

A black marlin leaps high out of the water. Its power and shape make it one of the high-speed swimmers of the ocean. Its snout is extended into a sharp spike, cutting through the water with little resistance, and its streamlined body tapers gently until it meets the curved tail. To feed, it dives into shoals of fish, attacking them at speed with remarkable precision.

GENTLE GIANT

Despite its huge size, the humpback whale is completely harmless to humans. At 16 metres (52 ft) in length, and weighing in at a hefty 65 tonnes, it is a graceful swimmer, using its large flippers to move its huge bulk with ease. Humpback whales are baleen whales, because of the bristles, or baleen, that hang in rows from the top of their mouths. The baleen acts as a strainer, trapping food, such as small fish or krill, after the whale has expelled a huge mouthful of water.

UNDERWATER GARDENS

Coral reefs teem with life. They grow only in warm water that is clean, shallow and with sufficient light. The majority of reefs are found around the tropics, where there is a rocky platform not too far below the surface. Many of the fish that live among the corals have flat bodies, which allow them to swim into, or through, the reef's many cracks and crevices.

OCEANS OF THE WORLD

There are five oceans around the world – the Pacific, Atlantic, Indian, Southern and Arctic Oceans – all linked together to form a single, large mass of salt water. The oceans are joined to seas, but these cover a smaller area than the oceans and are shallower. The Mediterranean, for example, a large inland sea between southern Europe and North Africa, is linked to the Atlantic Ocean by the Strait of Gibraltar. The oceans affect the weather and climate. The gravity of the Sun and Moon cause the tides. Ocean currents have an important influence on the movement of plankton and large marine animals.

THE ATLANTIC OCEAN

The Atlantic Ocean is the second largest ocean in the world. It separates North and South America in the west, from Europe and Africa in the east. A current, called the Gulf Stream, carries warm water from the tropics northwards to the coast of Norway, where it stops the sea from freezing. Underneath the ocean is a vast mountain range called the Mid-Atlantic Ridge, which is longer than the Himalayas.

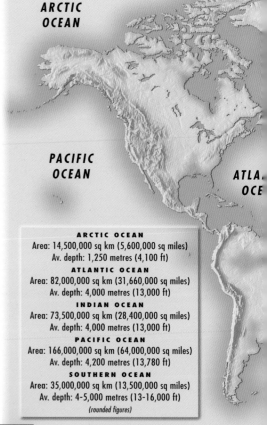

ARCTIC OCEAN

PACIFIC OCEAN

ATLA. OCE

ARCTIC OCEAN
Area: 14,500,000 sq km (5,600,000 sq miles)
Av. depth: 1,250 metres (4,100 ft)
ATLANTIC OCEAN
Area: 82,000,000 sq km (31,660,000 sq miles)
Av. depth: 4,000 metres (13,000 ft)
INDIAN OCEAN
Area: 73,500,000 sq km (28,400,000 sq miles)
Av. depth: 4,000 metres (13,000 ft)
PACIFIC OCEAN
Area: 166,000,000 sq km (64,000,000 sq miles)
Av. depth: 4,200 metres (13,780 ft)
SOUTHERN OCEAN
Area: 35,000,000 sq km (13,500,000 sq miles)
Av. depth: 4-5,000 metres (13-16,000 ft)
(rounded figures)

THE SOUTHERN OCEAN

Formed by the southern reaches of the Pacific, Atlantic and Indian Oceans, this ocean surrounds Antarctica, a large area of snow and ice-covered land at the South Pole. The rich, chilly water supports a wide variety of life, including this crabeater seal, which has jagged teeth for sieving krill, the small, shrimp-like creatures on which it feeds.

THE ARCTIC OCEAN

The Arctic is a partly-frozen ocean that lies to the north of North America, Asia and Europe. In the summer months, much of the pack ice melts, reducing the area covered by sea ice. In addition, great chunks of ice plunge into the sea from the ends of glaciers around Greenland, and float away as towering icebergs.

THE PACIFIC OCEAN

This is the largest and deepest of the oceans, with an area that is more than double that of the Atlantic Ocean. 'Pacific' means peaceful but, in fact, this ocean has some of the most violent sea and weather conditions of anywhere in the world, with destructive tropical storms and tsunamis (tidal waves). These are caused by volcanic activity and earthquakes on the ocean bed.

ARCTIC OCEAN

PACIFIC OCEAN

INDIAN OCEAN

SOUTHERN OCEAN

THE INDIAN OCEAN

This is an ocean of extremes, with a climate that ranges from warm and tropical in the north, to icy-cold where it meets the waters of the Southern Ocean. Dotted across the ocean are groups of beautiful islands. This is Kaafu Atoll in the Maldives, part of a string of coral islands to the southwest of India.

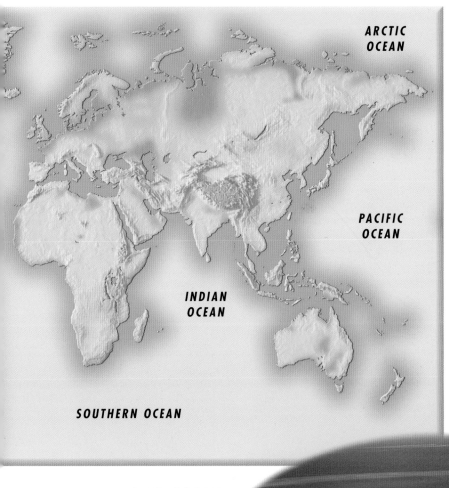

LAYERS OF LIFE

Scientists divide up the oceans into broad layers, or zones, so that if you took a trip down to the bottom of the ocean in a submersible (a type of deep-diving submarine) you would see the sunlit upper waters giving way to the twilight zone at about 200 metres (650 ft). Here the waters are poorly lit and the temperature of the water starts to drop rapidly. Below 1,000 metres (3,280 ft) you would enter the dark zone of the deep sea where no light penetrates. Deeper still are the abyss and the trenches. The Mariana Trench of the western Pacific is the deepest recorded sea trench at 11,034 metres (36,200 ft).

IN SHALLOW WATERS

Whether near the shore or out in the open ocean, animals and plants are most abundant in the well-lit shallow depths.

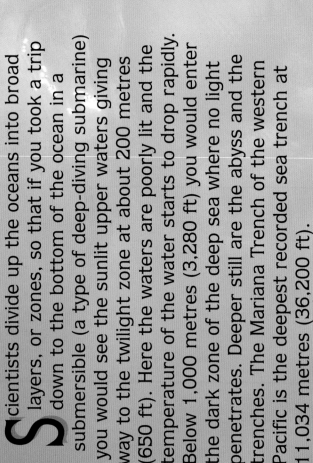
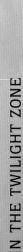

FLYING FISH

Out in the open ocean flying fish can be found, which can generate enough speed underwater to leap out of the water and, using their wing-like fins, glide through the air for 30 seconds or more to escape enemies.

IN THE TWILIGHT ZONE

Below the shallow waters are the shady depths of the twilight zone. Life is less common here compared to the sunlit upper waters, but still more abundant then the blackness of the deep ocean. Types of animals found here, such as these sponges, can also be seen at other depths. Sponges are not free-swimming but are attached to the same spot nearly all of their lives. Creatures such as these are called sessile animals.

THE DEEP OCEAN

Vents that spew out hot water rich in chemicals have been discovered in parts of the deep ocean floors of the Pacific and Atlantic Oceans. The brown-looking material is made up of microbes, called bacteria, which create food from the chemicals. These bacteria are, in turn, food for tube worms (the white animals) and other creatures.

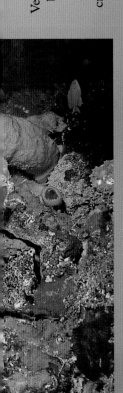

THE OCEAN DEPTHS

200 METRES

1000 METRES

4000 METRES

JOURNEY INTO THE DEEP

From the window of a submersible you would see how life changes as you descend. The clearly-lit surface reveals an abundance of life, with numerous fish, both small and large. But as you pass through the twilight zone, and you switch on your submersible's search lights, you would notice fewer and fewer fish swimming by. In the cold, black depths of the dark zone and beyond, the powerful beams show only fleeting glimpses of creatures. If you turned off the powerful lights you might see tiny, moving pinpoints of light – the light produced in the skin of some animals, called bioluminescence.

IN SUNLIT WATERS

The upper regions of the oceans are full of life. Here the sunlight is able to penetrate the water, providing the essential energy plants need to change the chemicals in the sea water into food in a process called photosynthesis. Apart from the community of animals that live around the deep ocean vents, the basis of the food chain for all the life in the oceans are the phytoplankton, microscopic plants which bloom in the sunlit waters. These are grazed on by tiny animals called zooplankton, which, in turn, are food for larger animals.

ZOOPLANKTON

Huge numbers of zooplankton float among the phytoplankton. These animals are joined by the larvae of crabs and lobsters, as well as molluscs, small shrimps and swimming crabs. They feed on the phytoplankton, on each other, or both. This drifting flourish of life is called plankton, and it forms a rich soup on which many creatures depend for their survival.

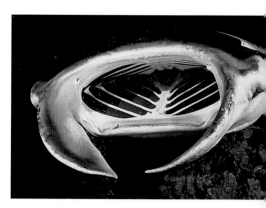

JELLYFISH

Jellyfish are invertebrates – creatures without a backbone. This compass jellyfish (left) floats near the surface of the ocean, often in large, wind-drifted groups near the coast. The long tentacles have stings for catching fish and other animals that stray into them. Some jellyfish are well known for their powerful stings. For example, the box jellyfish of Australasia can kill a person in less than five minutes. As a defence against the stings, Australian life guards used to wear outsize women's tights pulled up over their bodies.

FLOATING RAFTS OF WEED

Great yellowish rafts of Sargassum weed survive in the Sargasso Sea in the Atlantic Ocean, buoyed up by its small air bladders. The weed originally comes from weed beds in shallow, tropical waters. But during storms it floats out into the open ocean. Soon it begins to attract a wide variety of creatures.

PARROT FISH

A regal parrot fish nips off pieces of coral using its sharp, beak-like teeth, and then grinds up the hard mouthful with its back teeth to extract the polyps. Coral reefs are famed for their abundance of colourful fish. The bright hues make the fish stand out when they swim around the reef, but are good camouflage when they dive for safety among the corals themselves.

HEADS UP

Garden eels live in the huge expanses of sand that cover the ocean floor near the edges of the continents. They bury their tails in the sand and, with their heads held up, feed on particles of food carried in the currents that sweep across the sand.

WIDE-MOUTHED FISH

The manta ray's diet of plankton is so nourishing that it can grow to an incredible 7 metres (23 ft) across and weigh over 1.5 tonnes. On either side of its head are flipper-like scoops that channel the food into its wide mouth. The plankton are caught on combs as the water leaves its throat through slits on the sides of its head.

PACKED TOGETHER

A shoal of sardines feeds on the living broth of plankton. These and other small fish, such as herring, anchovy and flying fish, are hunted by marine predators, including mackerel, which are only slightly bigger than their prey. By swimming together the sardines follow one another in their search for food-rich waters. Large shoals also make it difficult for hunters to choose which fish to attack first.

THE TWILIGHT ZONE

The further you descend, the darker and colder the oceans get. The light fades rapidly and soon it becomes close to freezing. Algae do not grow here, so food is scarce. But there is a steady rain of debris – the bodies of creatures and droppings – drifting slowly downwards from the surface, and this provides a ready meal for the zooplankton, prawns and fish living in this twilight zone. Many creatures have developed large eyes so that they can see in the dim light, and their bodies are often coloured red, drab brown or black, providing excellent camouflage in the gloom. Most creatures also produce their own light, generated by light-producing organs called photophores. Sometimes the lights are on the underside of their bodies so that the creatures are less visible. Some animals spend the hours of daylight in the safety of the twilight zone, but come up to shallower waters to feed at night.

SPONGES

These sponges live on the bottom of the oceans. They filter out food particles by drawing in water through small pores and passing it out through larger holes. Food becomes scarcer and scarcer the deeper you go. With so little nourishment available, it can take a long time for the deeper-dwelling animals to grow to full maturity.

DAGGER TOOTHED

The viperfish's mouth has dagger-like teeth for grabbing its prey. The lower jaw is bigger than the top jaw, because the bottom teeth are so long – in fact, they do not fit into the mouth when it is closed. Inside the mouth are light organs which the fish uses to lure its prey to its death. The jaws hinge open very wide to allow the fish to swallow its meal.

SQUIDS

These torpedo-shaped animals are among the most common creatures living in the sea. This one has organs along its body to light its way in the deep water. Because of the huge pressure of the water on the bodies of creatures that live far below the surface, many of them are small. However, there are exceptions: the giant squid, which lives at depths of up to 1,000 metres (3,280 ft), can grow up to 20 metres (66 ft) long.

SEA LILY

At first sight you might be mistaken in believing that this was a plant. In fact, it is an animal, called a crinoid, or sea lily. Its delicate 'leaves' are feathery arms encircling the mouth. This one is on a shallow coral reef, but others are found at much greater depths, living in the deep sea and trenches.

BOGGLE EYES & WIDE MOUTH

The hatchet fish is so-called because of its deep belly, which gives it the appearance of a small axe. The bulbous eyes are specially designed for seeing in the extremely poor light, and are many times more sensitive to light than the human eye. Some hatchet fish look upwards, hoping to see the outline of their prey against the light from above, and then catch it in their wide mouths. Right is the skeleton of a hatchet fish, with its bones stained red.

THE DEEP OCEAN

No light from the Sun ever reaches below 1,000 metres (3,280 ft). Consequently, it is completely black. Since much of the rain of debris is eaten higher up, there is hardly any food and so there are fewer animals at the greater depths. The abyssal plain, down to 6,000 metres (19,690 ft), is covered in a layer of ooze. This mud-like carpet can be very thick – several hundred metres deep in some places – and is very soft. Scattered on some parts of the ocean floor are nodules – hard, round lumps of minerals, such as manganese, nickel and iron. Some are the size of cherries, others as large as grapefruits. They are not washed there by the currents, but form in very deep water. The nodules are valuable, and humans try to extract them by dredging.

ANGLER FISH

This ferocious-looking fish with its sharp teeth and wide gape has a lure on the top of its head. The lure is on a long spine, and its glow tempts other fish to thinking it is food. If one is foolish enough to be attracted by the lure, the angler fish quickly sucks it up whole into its large mouth. A female angler fish is up to 20 times larger than the male fish. In order to mate, the small male uses his teeth to attach himself to her body close to her reproductive opening. Remarkably, his body begins to fuse with her body, and eventually his heart wastes away as his bloodstream is replaced by hers. He is no longer able to swim away but is attached forever, fertilizing her eggs for the rest of her life.

MOUTH FOR GULPING

The gulper eel lives up to its name. To catch its prey, it swims slowly through the inky blackness with its gaping mouth open wide. When it runs into a small fish or shrimp, it immediately snaps its mouth shut and gulps down its prey before it has time to escape.

FISH WITH STILTS

The tripod fish has a special adaptation for its life at the bottom of the ocean – long stilts for standing or moving across the ooze. The thin stilts are like stiff filaments – one each on its two pelvic fins and one on its tail fin, making a tripod – which help the fish to stay clear of the soft ooze and to move along without stirring up the bottom into clouds of particles. The fish also has long antennae to help it 'see' in the dark.

DELICATE BASKET

This picture shows the skeleton of the fragile venus flower basket sponge, which dwells on the bottom of the ocean. It is found in colonies and grows up to 30 cm (12 inches) long.

BRITTLE STARFISH

These five-legged animals are found crawling on the bottom of both shallow and deep waters. Their arms are thin and very fragile and easily break off, hence their name. However, the starfish is able to grow new arms. It uses its arms to collect food fragments as they drift by.

RAT-TAIL FISH

This little fish gets its name from its long, thin body and tail. Fish living at great depths are often small and delicate. One reason for this is the scarcity of food and nutrients needed for growth. The rat-tail fish lives well below the strong ocean currents where the water is still, so it has little need for a powerful body for swimming. Hence it has developed its characteristic long, tail-like shape.

SEA CUCUMBER

Sea cucumbers are slug-like animals, which live in both deep and shallow waters. They crawl along the bottom of the seas and oceans, munching their way through the sediment in their quest to find particles of food. Some deep-sea cucumbers have long tube feet to help them walk through the soft ooze.

IN THE DARK

The deep ocean is a very inhospitable place: no sunlight ever reaches below 1,000 metres (3,280 ft), the temperature of the water is icy cold, food is scarce and the pressure of thousands of tonnes of water is so great, it would crush a diver in an instant should he go that deep. The animals that live here have special adaptations to allow them to survive the harsh conditions. For example, many deep-sea predators have massive mouths for catching prey (often several times larger than themselves) and stomachs that can stretch to take the huge meals. This is necessary because encounters between animals at great depths are few, and every opportunity for a meal must be taken, however large.

COLOURED GLASS

The fabulous glass jellyfish puts on a colourful display of rainbow colours. It can be found drifting in all the oceans of the world, from the sunlit surface waters down to the twilight zone. It has a transparent body shaped like a dome, and an opening that takes in food and passes out waste.

A FEROCIOUS BITE

The wicked-looking teeth of this deep-sea fish are not for ripping massive chunks out of its prey. Instead they are for trapping an unfortunate fish inside its cavernous mouth. They are bent backwards, allowing a fish to pass easily into the mouth. If its prey is very large – perhaps even larger than itself – it might not be able to close its mouth properly. Then the teeth act as a barrier, preventing the luckless fish from escaping.

NATURAL LIGHT

In the deep, dark depths
the only natural light you will
see is from the creatures that live
there. In nearly all cases the glow
comes from the photophores in
their bodies. The fact that so many animals of the deep have these
light organs shows that light plays a crucial role in their
survival. They can be used to attract or locate prey
or a mate, or to confuse an enemy. Common sites
for the organs are on the side of the head, on the
flank, on the underside of the body, or on
the end of a fin ray.

HAPPY GO LUCKY

Because of their large
mouths and strange shape,
many of the carnivorous fish found
in the deep look extremely odd.
Below the twilight zone, few fish have
swim bladders. These are air-filled
sacs that allow fish to regulate their
buoyancy, so that when they stop
swimming they neither sink nor
float upwards. Instead, deep ocean
fish achieve 'neutral buoyancy', largely
through having thin, lightweight skeletons
and muscles. They are small, too, many
no more than 10cm (4 inches) long. In the
tremendous pressure of the still water they
appear to hover when not swimming.

SCARLET PRAWN

Where a tiny amount of light still reaches the
depths, prawns are deep red in colour. In the
sunlit waters, their colour would make them stand
out and they would be easy prey for a hungry fish. But in
the lower reaches of the twilight zone, the redness of the
prawn's body is effective camouflage; in the dim light,
red appears black, so that the prawn blends into
the background. Below the twilight zone prawns
are nearly colourless – the blanket of blackness
hides them from their predators and so
there is no need for camouflage.

UNDERSEA GARDENS

In the sunlit waters of the oceans grow 'gardens' of seaweed. Seaweed is, in fact, algae. On land, algae grow in damp or wet areas and are small. But in the oceans they are in their element. The water supports the stipe (stem) and fronds (leaves) of the seaweed, allowing some types to grow to an enormous size. Most seaweeds anchor themselves to rock by root-like holdfasts, which grow into every crack in the rock. The holdfasts prevent them from being carried away by the waves. Seaweeds are home to a large array of creatures, including fish, crabs, shrimps and sea urchins.

FAN WORM

There are many marine animals that look rather like plants and the fan worm is one of them. It uses the tentacles of the fan to ensnare particles of food drifting in the water.

SEAWEED ZONES

Like plants on land, seaweeds need light in order to grow. Because of this they are found only in the sunlit waters. The colour of seaweeds gives an indication of their depth. Near the surface grow bright green seaweeds, such as sea lettuce. Then come greenish-brown seaweeds, such as the wracks, followed by brown kelp and then the red seaweeds.

ALL WRAPPED UP

The sea otter is a familiar inhabitant of the kelp beds of the Pacific Coast of North America, where they dive for food, such as shellfish, crustaceans and sea urchins. The sea otter collects the food and brings it to the surface where, using a stone as an anvil, it repeatedly bashes the shell until it cracks open and the otter is able to eat the tasty flesh inside. When it wants to sleep, the sea otter rolls over and over in the kelp until it is wrapped around its body. The kelp stops the sea otter from drifting away on the tide or with the wind.

KELP FORESTS

This diver is swimming through a forest of kelp off the coast of California. These large brown seaweeds, found in cold seas, can grow to lengths of over 60 metres (197 ft), providing shelter for the animals that live among them. Unlike land plants, kelp and other seaweeds have no need for roots; they are able to absorb all the water and nutrients they need from the sea around them. The holdfast's function is simply to fix the seaweed to the rock.

THE COW OF THE SEA

Dugongs are also called sea cows because they graze on the sea grasses that grow around the warm, shallow waters of the Indian and Pacific Oceans. They can grow to 3.6 metres (12 ft) long. They are the only vegetarian sea mammals and are very shy. From a distance, early sailors thought dugongs looked human-like, giving rise to stories about mermaids.

SEAWEEDS

SEA LETTUCE

WRACK

BROWN KELP

RED SEAWEED

CORAL REEFS

Coral reefs are found in warm, clear tropical waters. The reef is made by coral polyps, small anemone-like creatures that filter the water for food. Each polyp builds itself a protective outer skeleton to live in from a substance called calcium carbonate (or limestone). As it grows it develops a filament from which sprouts another polyp, which also builds a protective skeleton for itself. Gradually, the reef grows upwards and outwards, the outer layer being made of living coral growing on the skeletons of dead members of the colony. Living within the polyps are tiny algae, which are essential for the polyps' growth. The algae depend on the Sun for photosynthesis, so coral reefs do not grow below about 150 metres (490 ft). A great many creatures make their homes in or on the reef, creating one of the richest wildlife communities found anywhere in nature.

HARD CORAL   SOFT CORAL

HARD & SOFT

There are both hard corals, made by polyps with a hard outer skeleton, and soft corals, built by polyps with a hard internal skeleton. The strange shapes of reef corals give rise to some equally strange names: stag's horn, brain, sea fan, dead man's fingers and organ coral, for example. Corals come in many different colours. Hard corals, such as stag horn, are white because of their hard outer skeletons. But the soft corals are often brightly coloured yellow, red, green, black or blue.

DEADLY BEAUTY

Do not touch this attractive fish – it is one of the most poisonous creatures in the sea. The lionfish's lacy spines house venom which can leave nasty and painful wounds. The splendid display is a warning to predators not to tamper with the fish.

REEF BUILDING

Erskine Reef is part of the Great Barrier Reef, which stretches for 2,000 km (1,200 miles) down the northeast coast of Australia. It was built by creatures the size of a pinhead over a period of several million years. The small, low island, called a cay, is made up of fragments of coral. In the Pacific, reefs often form a ring around volcanic islands. These are called fringing reefs and the water inside the reefs is called a lagoon. Atolls are circular reefs or strings of coral islands surrounding a lagoon.

TINY TENTACLES

Coral polyps have tentacles with which to catch plankton. The tentacles, which form rings around the mouth of the animal, have darts which sting their prey. During the day, the stalks of the polyps are retracted into the protective skeletons, making the coral look like dead rock. At night they spread their tentacles to feed.

RECORD BREAKER

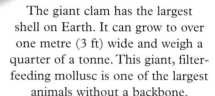

The giant clam has the largest shell on Earth. It can grow to over one metre (3 ft) wide and weigh a quarter of a tonne. This giant, filter-feeding mollusc is one of the largest animals without a backbone.

CROWN-OF-THORNS

This large, spiky-looking starfish feeds on the coral polyps. It does a great deal of damage and has destroyed large areas of Australia's Great Barrier Reef.

FOOD CHAIN

GREAT WHITE SHARK

TUNA

ANCHOVIES

ZOOPLANKTON

PHYTOPLANKTON

At the top of the marine food chain are the large hunters, such as sharks. These eat large fish that catch smaller fish, which in turn rely on zooplankton. The zooplankton eat the phytoplankton. Therefore the small plants that make food through photosynthesis are the basis of all life in the oceans.

PREDATORS & PREY

JET POWERED

Scallops have a unique way of escaping the deadly clutches of a hungry starfish. They use jet power to launch themselves off the bottom of the ocean, and swim away by squeezing a jet of water out of their shells. Unlike most other molluscs of their type, scallops do not bury themselves in the sand or fix themselves to the rocky bed, and so are able to escape a marauding predator.

The deadly game of attack and defence is played out at every level of the ocean. Creatures are constantly on the lookout for prey. But there is no such thing as an easy meal, for no creature – however large or small – wants to end up as lunch for another animal. Some animals, such as the poisonous lionfish have bright warning colours that tell a predator to keep clear of its poisonous spines. But other animals must take evasive action if they are to survive an attack.

NO ESCAPE

Even the stinging cells on the tentacles of the jelly-like *Porpita* are no defence against the sea slug, *Glaucus*, a type of shell-less mollusc (left). The sea slug crawls along the underside of the water surface looking for *Porpita*, and when it finds one it immediately starts feeding on it, stings and all.

DEADLY EMBRACE

The flower-like sea anemone, with its colourful 'petals', looks pretty and innocent. But any small fish that comes too close had better beware, for the petals are armed with poisonous stinging cells. Once caught in its deadly embrace, the poor fish is pulled towards the anemone's mouth in the centre of the ring of tentacles.

UNDERWATER FLIGHT

Many sea birds dive into the water to catch a meal, but the Galapagos penguin chases fish underwater, using its flipper-like wings to propel it through the water at speed. When fish swim in shoals, they may confuse the bird, preventing it from deciding on a catch. The flashing of their silvery bodies may also confuse the penguin for a moment, allowing the fish to escape.

KILLER ON THE ATTACK

On an Argentinian beach a killer whale attacks sea lions by charging at them in the shallows. The killer whale, an air-breathing mammal, is willing to almost beach itself in order to catch its prey. This 10-metre (33-ft) predator is the only whale to prey on other whales.

TERROR OF THE OCEANS

The most feared fish in the ocean is the great white shark. This eating machine prefers seals, turtles and large fish, but occasionally has been known to attack humans, its sharp teeth leaving terrible injuries. The shark's streamlined body shape allows it to swim effortlessly through the water, driven by its large, powerful tail. Sharks have no swim bladder so they must swim constantly to stay afloat.

MIGRATION

Animals that move from one place to another are said to migrate. For example, zooplankton make a daily migration. During the night they feed on the phytoplankton that live in the surface waters. But as day breaks they swim down several hundred metres to escape hungry predators. However, for other marine animals, migration is more commonly associated with breeding. Some fish, seals, whales and turtles make spectacular migrations, often swimming thousands of kilometres on difficult journeys to lay their eggs or give birth to their offspring. They travel to a place where the young have the best chance of survival, perhaps where there are plentiful food supplies, guided on their journey by the ocean currents.

THE CONGER EEL

The conger eel of the North Atlantic is a fearless hunter. It has rows of sharp, backward-pointing teeth that grip into its prey. The only known spawning ground of the conger eel is north of the Azores. It seems that all western European congers travel here in mid-summer to lay their eggs, later returning to colder northern waters.

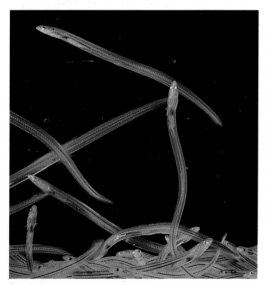

MIGRATION MYSTERY

The mystery of the European eel's breeding habits remained a puzzle until this century. Then it was discovered that the adult eels leave the rivers of Europe and swim out into the Sargasso Sea in the Atlantic Ocean, where they spawn and then die. After about three years, the young eels, or elvers, find their way to these rivers, where they remain until they, too, are ready to return to the spawning grounds in the Atlantic.

TURTLE TRAVELS

Green turtles come ashore to lay their eggs. But they do not breed on any beach they come across. Instead they travel hundreds, even thousands, of kilometres to the place where they hatched. Under the cover of darkness, they haul themselves high up the beach, where they use their large, powerful flippers to dig a deep nest in the soft sand. After carefully covering the eggs with sand, the females return to the sea to leave the young to fend for themselves.

WHALE OF A TIME

A southern right whale surfaces in the food-rich waters of the Southern Ocean. When it is time for the females to give birth, they migrate north to the warmer waters of their breeding grounds. There is not much food there, so the adults must survive on their reserves of blubber until they are able to return to their feeding grounds.

MARCHING IN SINGLE FILE

The spiny lobster lives close to the coast where the ocean bed is rocky. For most of the year, they hide in crevices during the day, venturing out at night to feed on worms and dead animals. But in the autumn, along the Florida coast of the USA and the Caribbean, their behaviour changes. They join together in long queues of up to 50 lobsters, each one keeping in touch with the lobster in front of it with its long antennae. They move off away from the coast into deep water, where they mate.

PRAWN LARVAE

A female prawn, called *Parapandalus*, carries her eggs stuck to her legs on the underside of her body. It lives at depths of about 500-700 metres (1,640-2,300 ft) in the dim regions of the ocean. When the eggs hatch, the larvae swim up to the surface to feed on the phytoplankton. As they grow, they change their diet and start to eat other small animals. They eventually migrate down to the depths where the adults live.

SPAWN & YOUNG

A MERMAID'S PURSE

This is the name for the dried-out, empty egg cases of skates, rays and dogfish, often found washed up on the beach. Here a swell shark embryo sits on its egg case. The male fertilized the female and when the eggs developed she laid the egg cases, attaching them to seaweed by tendrils at each corner. The embryos live off the yolk sac until they have developed enough to emerge.

Many marine animals do not have elaborate courtship behaviour or care for their young. When the time is right, the female simply releases her eggs into the water while the male fertilizes them with his sperm. The eggs are left to develop on their own, and when they hatch the young grow and develop without the help of their parents. However, the eggs and young are food for a great many animals. So hundreds, even thousands, of eggs are often laid by one animal in order that at least a few individuals survive to adulthood and are able to spawn (produce eggs) themselves. There are some exceptions to this rule. Like other mammals, whales are good examples of animals that take good care of their young. When they are born, the calves are helped to the surface to take their first breath. They drink their mothers' milk for many months and are protected from predators by the adults.

DESPERATE DASH

Loggerhead turtle hatchlings head for the relative safety of the ocean. The mother loggerhead laid her eggs in the sand about two months earlier. As the babies emerge from the sand, it is the most dangerous part of their young lives, for they are easy prey for sea birds, crabs and other predators.

So as soon as they hatch, they scramble as fast as possible to the ocean. One day they will return to the beach where they were born to lay eggs of their own.

BRAIN SPAWN

Coral reefs start when tiny planktonic larvae settle in warm, shallow water where they become polyps . The larvae develop when a coral, such as this brain coral, releases packets of eggs and sperm into the water.

PUPPY LOVE

Not all fish lay eggs. Some sharks do lay eggs, but most sharks breed like whales and other mammals and give birth to live young. After mating with the male, the female carries an embryo which develops inside her body. When it is fully formed she gives birth to the infant shark, which looks exactly like an adult but much smaller. Here a lemon shark pup is being born.

ROLE REVERSAL

Unusually, it is the male sea horse that becomes pregnant and gives birth to the young. The female lays her eggs in a pouch in the male's body, using a tube called an ovipositor, and then leaves him to look after them. Several weeks later the baby sea horses hatch and are ready to be born. Then the male begins to convulse forwards and backwards, and with each backwards movement a baby shoots out of the pouch. He gives birth to around 200 baby sea horses.

SOLE METAMORPHOSIS

When a sole is born it swims like other fish and has an eye on each side of its head. As it grows, one eye starts to move around its head so that by the time it is an adult, both eyes are on the same side of its body and it is able to swim flat on the sea bed.

TEN DAYS OLD

THIRTEEN DAYS OLD

TWENTY-TWO DAYS OLD

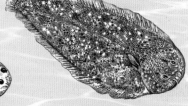

ADULT SOLE

LIVING TOGETHER

MATING GAME

A large school of squid torpedoes around in order to find a mate. These fast-moving animals hunt together, using their large eyes to seek out a shoal of fish. The squids use their 10 sucker-covered tentacles to grasp their prey – or a mate. Squids can move forwards or backwards through the water. They have two methods of propulsion. With the first, the squid sucks water into its body and then squirts it out of a tube at high speed; the force of the water-jet shoots it through the ocean. The second method is slower: the squid moves by waving the fin at the rear of its body.

Throughout the oceans, there are creatures that live together, often forming close relationships. These relationships do not happen by chance – there is always a reason for them. Some animals of the same kind band together and swim in large shoals as a defence against predators, or to improve their chances of catching a meal. Other relationships involve animals of very different kinds, each creature providing some form of benefit for the other. This type of relationship is called 'symbiosis'. In the case of coral polyps, the symbiotic relationship is between the polyps and the algae living within them.

CLOWNING AROUND

A clownfish finds refuge among the stinging tentacles of a sea anemone that would paralyse other fish in seconds: the clownfish's body is covered in a mucus that renders it immune to the sea anemone's stings. In return, the sea anemone benefits from the bits that are left over from its guest's meal, or by capturing predators that are drawn to attack the clownfish and instead end up in the anemone's deadly embrace.

HAPPY HERMIT

This hermit crab crawls along the sea bed. The shell in which it is living, and which protects its soft, vulnerable body, once belonged to a mollusc. And on the shell it has placed anemones whose stinging tentacles provide the hermit crab with protection against its predators. In return, the anemones get to feed on food particles left over from the crab's meals.

FLOATING FLOTSAM

Living among the floating Sargassum weed and drifting with it are many different animals, including sea slugs, crabs, shrimps and goose barnacles, all cleverly adapted to their special habitat. Here a small fish with fleshy growths blends in with the weed, making it almost invisible to predators. A sea anemone sits nearby, waiting for a fish to swim into its stinging tentacles. Both creatures are using colour as camouflage, allowing them to blend in with the weed.

CLEANING SERVICE

Cleaner wrasses give the inside of a large cod's mouth a wash and brush up without being harmed. The wrasses help the cod (and other fish) by removing parasites or particles of food; in return they get a free meal.

HITCHING A RIDE

A remora hitches a ride on a manta ray. The remora has a sucker on the top of its head which it uses to attach itself to the larger fish. Remoras are often seen on sharks, disengaging themselves to feed on the scraps of a kill.

PEOPLE & THE OCEAN

TOURIST TRAP

A scuba diver admires the inhabitants of a coral reef. Foreign holidays in the sun are now immensely popular, with the majority of people visiting destinations on the coast. Sun bathing, fishing trips, sailing and diving are just a few of the popular activities on offer at holiday resorts. While tourism brings welcome money for the local population and a better standard of living, it does have its dangers for the environment.

People have always been involved with the oceans, depending on them at first for food, and then later for mineral wealth. People have fished for thousands of years, and today it remains a major occupation in both the developing world and richer countries. Mining of the sea is important too. For example, the age-old extraction of salt from sea water has been joined by the dredging of sand and gravel, and the drilling for oil and gas (shown here). Tourism has become a major industry too, and in many traditional coastal communities this has replaced fishing as the main source of income.

FISH HARVEST

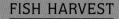

This Scottish fishing boat is bringing its catch aboard. Day and night, large fishing boats all round the world reap the bounty of the oceans in an attempt to satisfy the rising demand for fish. With more powerful boats, improved technology and bigger nets, they are able to remain at sea for longer, and bring home bigger catches. In order to avoid overfishing and depleting stocks of fish, there are international treaties which set precise limits on the size of a country's catch.

DIVING FOR PEARLS

A pearl diver in Thailand brings his catch of oysters to the surface. The pearls are formed around a foreign body, such as a grain of sand, inside the shell of an oyster or mussel, and take several years to grow. Pearl diving is difficult and dangerous work. This diver is using make-shift diving equipment made from a generator and some rubber tubing. Pearls are much valued as gems and so the money the diver earns from selling them makes the job worth the risk.

STILT FISHERMEN

In traditional societies methods of fishing have not changed in hundreds of years. Here a Sri Lankan fisherman perches patiently on his stilt while waiting for a bite. For people in coastal villages in poor countries, the oceans are often the only source of food. For many people it is their livelihood, but often it is under threat from foreign fishing boats that take the local fish stocks.

PROTECTING THE REEFS & OCEANS

Unfortunately, people repeatedly fail to realize the effect of their actions on the environment. This has been especially the case with the oceans for, being so large, they have been treated carelessly. Poison waste dumped at sea filters into the food chain, eventually affecting life at all levels of the oceans. Having no real boundaries, the effects of harming them can spread well beyond the local environment. But through public awareness of the issues, progress has been made in protecting the oceans. For example, an action agenda, called Agenda 21, has been agreed by world leaders. This sets out key ways in which countries can manage the marine environment.

WHALE-WATCHING

Tourism has even reached the cold waters of the Southern Ocean. Here a group of sightseers in an inflatable dinghy get a wonderful view of a humpback whale performing its aquabatics. Whale-watching has become a popular and novel form of tourism, but if left unregulated there may be a danger that boat operations could interfere with the whales' everyday lives, especially during times of mating. If the whales feel harassed, they might abandon their traditional breeding sites because it would no longer be safe there, and that would spell disaster for the future of these majestic mammals.

TURTLE HATCHERY

In many countries, turtle eggs are a delicacy. On the nights when the animals come ashore to breed, local people patrol the beaches and collect the eggs for sale in the local markets. Some countries have made an effort to protect the eggs. In Sri Lanka, green turtle eggs are placed in a hatchery for protection and the baby turtles released directly into the ocean.

PROTECTING THE REEFS

Some coral reefs have been made marine nature reserves, to protect them from over-exploitation, such as the plundering of coral, sponges and shells for sale to tourists, or the collection of fish for pet-shops. People have found other ways of developing tourism in these places, creating local jobs without harming the delicate reef environment.

DOLPHIN DELIGHT

Despite being wild, the bottlenose dolphins at Monkey Mia in Western Australia come into the shallows to seek human contact. This interaction allows us to study the wild dolphins, in the hope of understanding more about them. There are just under 40 species of dolphin, but several are threatened by fishing nets, over-fishing and pollution.

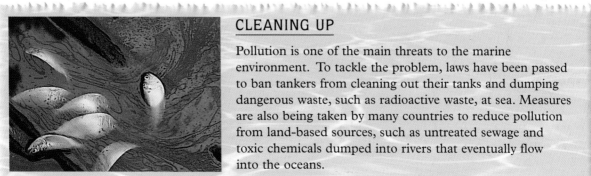

CLEANING UP

Pollution is one of the main threats to the marine environment. To tackle the problem, laws have been passed to ban tankers from cleaning out their tanks and dumping dangerous waste, such as radioactive waste, at sea. Measures are also being taken by many countries to reduce pollution from land-based sources, such as untreated sewage and toxic chemicals dumped into rivers that eventually flow into the oceans.

THE LIVING FOREST

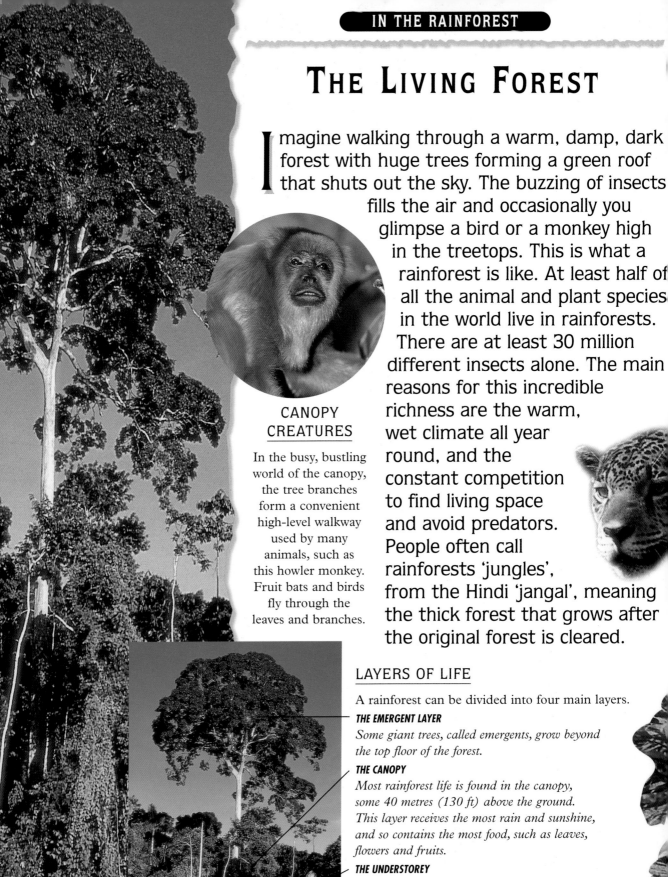

Imagine walking through a warm, damp, dark forest with huge trees forming a green roof that shuts out the sky. The buzzing of insects fills the air and occasionally you glimpse a bird or a monkey high in the treetops. This is what a rainforest is like. At least half of all the animal and plant species in the world live in rainforests. There are at least 30 million different insects alone. The main reasons for this incredible richness are the warm, wet climate all year round, and the constant competition to find living space and avoid predators. People often call rainforests 'jungles', from the Hindi 'jangal', meaning the thick forest that grows after the original forest is cleared.

CANOPY CREATURES

In the busy, bustling world of the canopy, the tree branches form a convenient high-level walkway used by many animals, such as this howler monkey. Fruit bats and birds fly through the leaves and branches.

LAYERS OF LIFE

A rainforest can be divided into four main layers.

THE EMERGENT LAYER
Some giant trees, called emergents, grow beyond the top floor of the forest.

THE CANOPY
Most rainforest life is found in the canopy, some 40 metres (130 ft) above the ground. This layer receives the most rain and sunshine, and so contains the most food, such as leaves, flowers and fruits.

THE UNDERSTOREY
Between the canopy and the forest floor is an understorey of smaller trees, climbing plants and large-leaved shrubs that can tolerate the shade.

THE FOREST FLOOR
Only one or two per cent of the sunlight that hits the canopy filters through to the forest floor. The ground is almost bare except for a thin carpet of leaves.

FOREST GIANTS

The year-round warmth of the rainforest has allowed some animals to grow into giants, such as the giant millipedes. These look rather alarming but actually feed on dead plant material. Other rainforest giants include the largest frog in the world, the goliath frog, and the largest butterfly, the Queen Alexandra's birdwing butterfly.

FOREST PEOPLES

This Kalapolo Indian lives in the Brazilian rainforest. People have inhabited rainforests for thousands of years, but little is known of their origins, their relationship to one another, nor how they colonized the forest. Warmth and moisture break down organic materials, such as wood, very quickly, so ancient remains are rare.

LIFE IN THE UNDERSTOREY

Among the tangle of leaves and branches in the understorey live climbing and grasping animals. Many are small and light, such as tree frogs, lemurs, coatis and tree snakes like this emerald tree boa. Others are much heavier and have to keep to the larger branches.

THE FOREST FLOOR

Large hunters such as jaguars and tigers prowl along the forest floor. Hogs, peccaries and tapirs can root out bulbs and shoots from the soil, and there are plenty of insects for hungry giant anteaters and tenrecs.

RAINFORESTS OF THE WORLD

WHERE IN THE WORLD?

There are four main areas of rainforest in the world today – in Central and South America, in Africa, in Southeast Asia and in Australasia(all shaded dark green). Every rainforest in the world is different with many species of plants and animals living only in one area. This is because the continents have drifted apart over millions of years, separating the different areas of rainforest so that the plants and animals developed separately into different forms.

The word 'rain' forest was first used in 1898 to describe forests that grow in constantly wet conditions. Most rainforests have an annual rainfall of 250 cm (almost 100 inches), which is spread evenly throughout the year. Thunderstorms are common in the afternoons. Water given off by the trees adds to the moisture in the air, so the air feels sticky, or humid, and clouds and mist hang over the forest like smoke. This blanket of cloud protects the forest from daytime heat and night-time chill, keeping temperatures between 23 °C (73 °F) and 31 °C (88 °F) throughout the year. The hottest, wettest rainforests occur in a narrow belt around the Equator. These are sometimes called lowland rainforests and they are the most extensive. Rainforests further away from the Equator are just as warm as lowland rainforests, but have a short dry season. Another type of rainforest, called cloud forest, grows on tropical mountains, while mangrove rainforests grow on some tropical coasts.

RAINFOREST CLIMATE

Rainforests are hot because they grow in a band around the middle of the Earth where the Sun's rays are at their hottest and strongest. The Sun's heat warms the ground, which then warms the air above it. The warm air rises up. As it rises, it cools down and moisture in the air condenses into water droplets, which collect together to make clouds and rain.

COLD AIR

WARM AIR

EQUATOR

MONSOON OR SEASONAL FORESTS

Tropical rainforests with three or more dry months each year are called monsoon forests or seasonal forests. This is because the trees drop their leaves in the dry season and grow new leaves at the start of the wet monsoon season. These forests have fewer climbing plants than lowland rainforests because the air is drier. There are also more plants growing on the forest floor because a lot of light reaches the ground in the dry season.

CLOUD FORESTS

High up on tropical mountains – above 900 metres (3,000 ft) – grow misty forests of gnarled, twisted, stunted trees covered in bright green mosses and dripping with water. Lichens hang down like beards from the tree branches and ferns, orchids and other plants perch along the boughs. These cloud (or montane) forests have fewer plant species than lowland forests, as low temperatures and strong winds restrict plant growth.

MANGROVE FORESTS

Tropical shorelines are often clothed in a special type of rainforest, called a mangrove forest, which does not have a great variety of species. These forests grow on the coasts of the Indian Ocean, the western Pacific Ocean, and also on the shores of the Americas, the Caribbean and West Africa.

WHAT'S THE WEATHER?

Inside a rainforest, the local, or micro-climate, varies at different levels, so those animals on the forest floor experience different conditions to those in the canopy. When it rains, the water drips down through the leaves, sometimes taking 10 minutes to reach the ground. When the Sun shines, the air at the top of the canopy is hot and dry, but on the ground it is always warm and damp. A strong wind may be blowing up in the canopy, but at ground level there isn't even a breeze.

THE WATER CYCLE

As rain drips down through the rainforest, the trees and plants take in moisture through their leaves and roots. Unused water evaporates, or disappears, into the air through tiny holes in their leaves. Water also evaporates from the ground. All the warm, wet air rises up into the sky, where it cools down to make rain clouds. Rain falls down from the clouds into the forest to start the rainfall cycle all over again.

ASIAN RAINFORESTS

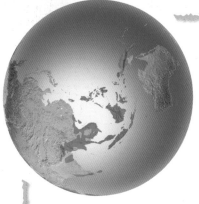

The main area of rainforest in Southeast Asia spreads down the mainland of Malaysia to Indonesia. Widespread human disturbance of the forests of mainland Southeast Asia has left little of the rainforest in its natural state. Some islands, such as the Philippines, have hardly any rainforest left. Because of this, many of the Asian rainforest species are in danger of extinction, such as the Sumatran rhino and the Vietnam pheasant. Other areas, such as Borneo, still have much of their original forest cover.

ASIAN FORESTS

Almost 40 per cent of all the rainforest in Asia is to be found in the Indonesian archipelago, and most of the richest mangrove forests occur along Southeast Asian coasts.

KING COBRA

The largest of all venomous, or poisonous, snakes, king cobras grow to a length of up to 5.5 metres (18 ft). They are actually shy snakes and prefer to keep well away from people. Female king cobras are the only snakes known to build a nest for their eggs.

MALAYAN TAPIR

The black and white colours of the Malayan tapir help to break up its outline so predators cannot see it in the dark. Tapirs are shy, timid, solitary animals and come out mainly at night. They use their long trunk like nose to pull tender shoots, buds and fruits from rainforest plants.

MANGROVE TREES

Mangrove trees grow in salty, silty mud and have a tangle of branching roots to support them in the waterlogged ground. Special breathing roots stick up through the mud into the air to help the roots get enough oxygen. The roots also trap the mud and help to stabilize the coastline and build up new strips of land.

ATLAS MOTH

This is one of the largest moths in the world. It has a wingspan of up to 30 cm (12 inches) and is often mistaken for a bird as it flutters around the rainforests of Southeast Asia. Males have huge feathery antennae – the largest of any butterfly or moth – to help them pick up the scent of females among the rainforest trees.

AUSTRALASIAN RAINFORESTS

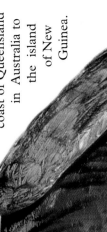

The largest expanse of rainforest in Australasia grows on the island of New Guinea. Most of it is still undisturbed and contains a mixture of Asian and Australasian plants and animals. Australian rainforests are all that remain of a vast rainforest that once covered parts of this continent and Antarctica during much warmer climates millions of years ago. They are not as rich in species as other rainforests but they contain many unique forms of life.

AUSTRALASIAN RAINFORESTS

Australasian rainforests spread up from the northeastern coast of Queensland in Australia to the island of New Guinea.

RAINBOW LORIKEET

Screeching flocks of rainbow lorikeets feed in the upper canopy, lapping up nectar and pollen from flowers with their brush-tipped tongues. They may have to fly long distances in search of flowering trees.

SPOTTED CUSCUS

Eight species of cuscus, including the spotted cuscus, occur in the rainforests of New Guinea. Cuscuses have a partly-bald prehensile tail for gripping branches. At night they feed on leaves, flowers and insects; some species feed in the rainforest canopy, others in the understorey or on the ground.

TREE KANGAROOS

Australasian rainforests do not have monkeys and apes climbing and swinging through the trees. Instead, they have tree kangaroos and a variety of marsupials, such as possums and gliders. Tree kangaroos occur mainly on New Guinea, but two species live in Queensland rainforests. Tree kangaroos are different from ground-dwelling kangaroos because they have powerful front legs, relatively short, broad back feet, sharp claws for gripping branches and a long, cylindrical tail. The long tail helps a tree kangaroo to balance on tree branches, and also acts as a rudder when it leaps from branch to branch.

AFRICAN RAINFORESTS

African rainforests contain fewer species than the rain-forests of either America or Asia. This is because many plants and animals died out when the climate of Africa became much drier during the last Ice Age, which ended about 12,000 years ago. Most of the wildlife in Madagascar's rainforests is unique to the island because it has evolved in isolation from Africa for at least 40 million years.

THE SAME BUT DIFFERENT

Animals living in rainforests in different parts of the world have sometimes come to look the same because they have adapted to a similar lifestyle. They are different species, but because they live, feed and survive in a similar way, their bodies look similar. This idea is called convergent evolution and some examples are the hornbills of Africa (above) and the toucans of South America (below).

COLOBUS MONKEY

Living in troops of over 50 animals made up of small family groups, black and white colobus monkeys are active during the daytime. They feed on bark, insects, fruit and leaves, leaping acrobatically from tree to tree. Unlike South American monkeys, African monkeys do not have prehensile, or gripping, tails.

GOLIATH BEETLE

The heaviest of all insects, male goliath beetles weigh from 70-100g (2.5-3.5 oz), which is roughly three times as much as a house mouse. From the tip of the small horns to the end of the abdomen, they are up to 11 cm (4 inches) long. Females are smaller than males.

AFRICAN FORESTS

A belt of tropical rainforest grows across the centre of Africa, from Cameroon and Gabon on the West African coast, to Kenya and Tanzania in East Africa. More than 80 per cent of Africa's rainforest is in central Africa. These forests spread out from small patches of forest that survived the dry African climate during the last Ice Age. In East Africa, rainforest grows mainly in mountain regions.

GREY PARROT

Noisy grey parrots whistle and shriek to each other before settling down to roost for the night in groups of 100 or more. They have remarkable powers of mimicry and captive birds can be trained to use human language as a means of communicating intelligently with people.

AMERICAN RAINFORESTS

By far the biggest area of rainforest is in the Amazon basin in South America. It is twice the size of India and ten times the size of France. About one-fifth of all the world's bird and flowering plant species and one tenth of all its mammal species live in the Amazon rainforest. Each type of tree may support more than 400 insect species.

YELLOW ANACONDA

The yellow anaconda is one of the heaviest snakes. It is highly aquatic, hunting fish and caimans in streams and rivers. Anacondas are a type of boa and constrict their prey, squeezing it to death in their strong coils.

BALD UAKARI

With its bare face and head, long shaggy fur and a beard, the bald uakari is a strange-looking monkey indeed. The three species of uakari are the only New World monkeys to have short tails. They rarely leap, because they do not have long tails to help them balance.

MORPHO BUTTERFLY

The shimmery blue colours on the wings of a male morpho butterfly help to attract females and may also serve to dazzle predators when the butterfly needs to escape. The colours are caused by the way the tiny scales on the wings reflect the light.

AMERICAN RAINFORESTS

The rainforests of the Americas range from the vast forests of the Amazon up through Central America and on to some of the islands in the Caribbean. These islands have many unusual species — some found on only one island. Hurricanes, however, often cause damage to the Caribbean rainforests. The relatively tiny rainforests of Central America are rich in species because they grow on a land bridge between two very different continents.

RAINFOREST PLANTS

Trees form the superstructure of a rainforest. Their crowns make roof gardens for perching plants; their mighty trunks support the weight of the canopy and provide climbing frames for rope-like creepers; and their roots help to hold the soil together. Rainforest trees are usually 30-50 metres (100-160 ft) tall, with slender, unbranched trunks, smooth bark and hard wood. Their life span can be from 150 years to 1,400 years. The leaves of rainforest trees, and other rainforest plants, are often thick and leathery with pointed tips called drip tips. The rain runs quickly off these leaves and stops moss from growing and blocking out the light. A rainforest has a huge variety of trees – an area the size of a soccer pitch could hold as many as 200 species.

A SAFE HAVEN

To get nearer to the light, many plants perch high on the branches of the tall trees. Some of these plants, called bromeliads, make a cup-shaped container with their waxy leaves, which can hold many gallons of water. Animals, like this frog, take advantage of these tree-top ponds as safe places for their young.

GROWING SPACE

One of the main problems for rainforest trees is finding a space in which to grow. Strangler figs have solved this problem by taking the place of a tree already standing.

A bird drops a strangler fig seed on a tree branch and the seed sprouts roots and branches.

The strangler's roots reach the ground and it starts to smother the host tree.

The host tree dies away, leaving the fig standing in its place.

STINKBIRDS

The hoatzin of South America smells rather like cow manure because its stomach is full of fermenting leaves. It is one of the few rainforest birds to feed on leaves, which stay in the hoatzin's stomach for almost two days, making it too heavy to be a good flier.

BUTTRESS ROOTS

The roots of some trees spread out above the ground to form wide, flat wings called buttresses. These buttress roots may extend 5 metres (16 ft) up the trunk. They probably help to support the tall trees, but may also help the tree to feed. They spread widely and send down fine feeding roots into the soil.

CARNIVOROUS PLANTS

Pitcher plants get extra nutrients by catching and digesting insects and other small animals. Some of the pitchers rest on the ground, while others hang like lanterns along the branches of supporting trees. Some even have lids to keep out the rain. Creatures are attracted by the glistening colours and sweet nectar produced around the rim of the pitcher, but fall down the slippery walls into a pool of acidic liquid. The liquid digests the animals' bodies and the plant absorbs the goodness they contain.

PARASITIC PLANTS

Plants need light to make food, but there is not much light on the dark forest floor. Some plants survive here by stealing their food from other plants. The biggest flower in the world, Rafflesia, is a parasitic plant like this. The body of the plant is a network of threads living inside the woody stems of a vine that hangs down from the trees and trails along the ground. The flower bud pushes its way out through the vine's bark and then expands to form a flower up to 1 metre (3 ft) across.

PLANT PARTNERS

AVOCADO BIRD

The resplendent quetzal feeds on at least 18 different species of avocado, and the trees and the birds need each other to survive. The quetzals swallow the avocado fruit whole but the hard seed passes through the bird's gut unharmed, or is regurgitated later. A new tree can grow from the seed, so the quetzal spreads avocado trees through the forest. If the avocado trees are cut down, or stop fruiting, the quetzals usually disappear from the area.

Most flowering plants in a rainforest need pollen from another plant of the same kind in order to produce seeds. There is very little wind, so they rely on animals to transport the pollen. Highly mobile animals, such as birds, bats and monkeys are useful for spreading seeds as they move over large areas of the forest. Flowers and seeds may sprout directly from trunks or branches to make contact more easily with bats and other large animals, without all the leaves getting in the way. Bat flowers tend to be large, pale and smelly sobats can find them in the dark, while bird flowers are brilliant colours because birds have good colour vision. Some insects, especially ants, have more complex relationships with rainforest plants – they live right inside the plants and help them to survive.

PERFUME FOR POLLEN

The bucket orchid of Central America goes to extraordinary lengths to make sure iridescent male bees carry its pollen from flower to flower. To lure the bees into its watery trap, the bucket orchid produces a perfume that the male bees use to attract female bees during courtship. While scraping perfume off the orchid's petals, the bees sometimes slip and fall down into the bucket.

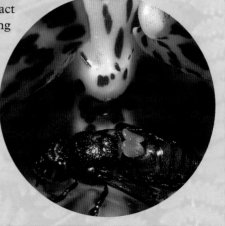

As they escape, they either pick up a new load of pollen or deposit pollen they are already carrying. The pollen is the two lumps stuck to the bee's back like a yellow rucksack (right).

SPREADING SEEDS

Living inside the stems, branches and even the leaves of several rainforest plants are colonies of ants. In exchange for their protected nesting place, the ants provide the plants with much needed nutrients in their droppings and the remains of their insect meals. Ant plants are often epiphytes, perched high on tree branches, so they cannot get nutrients from the soil to help them grow. The ants may also defend the plants by biting and stinging animals that try to eat them. This ant plant has holes in the surface of its swollen, prickly stem through which its ant lodgers scurry in and out of their living home. As the ants move about the forest, they help to spread the seeds of the ant plant.

GREEN FUR

The greenish tinge to the sloth's fur is provided by tiny plants called algae which live in grooves in the damp hair. Sloths never clean their fur so the algae do not get washed off, and they benefit by living high in the trees, near to the light. With green fur, sloths blend into the leafy green background of the forest so their plant hitchhikers camouflage them from predators. Another animal takes advantage of the sloth-algae relationship. A tiny moth lays it eggs in the sloth's green fur and its caterpillars seem to feed on the algae.

BEETLE MESSENGERS

To attract beetles for pollination, the *Philodendron* plant produces a powerful scent which travels great distances. The flowering spike even heats up to help the scent evaporate and disperse into the air. The beetles feed and mate inside the flower, then fly off covered with pollen to another *Philodendron* flower.

MOVING THROUGH THE TREES

FLYING LIZARD

In the Southeast Asian rainforests, lizards are some of the most common gliders. Their stiff gliding flaps are made of thin membranes of skin joined to their ribs. These lizards can glide for up to 15 metres (50 ft) between trees, and even change position and roll over while in the air. Gliders make easy targets for hungry birds so many are camouflaged or come out at night when it is harder for predators to see them on the move.

Even with special climbing equipment, people find it difficult and dangerous reaching the top of rainforest trees. Yet rainforest animals spend their lives swinging, climbing and gliding through the trees. Useful adaptations for these forest acrobats include long arms for swinging, tails for gripping, hanging and balancing, and sticky toes, rough soles or long claws for extra grip. Short, rounded wings help predatory birds to twist and turn through the branches while hummingbirds and moths hover in front of flowers like jet aircraft on their small, pointed wings. Some animals glide from tree to tree instead of leaping and travel long distances with very little effort. Webs or flaps of skin increase the surface area of the body and slow down the glider's fall, like a living parachute. There is even a flying snake which can glide for distances of more than 50 metres (165 ft).

CLINGING CLAWS

The long, strong claws of a sloth work like hooks to allow the animal to spend much of its time hanging upside down from the branches of trees – even when it is asleep or dead. The claws make a rigid, fixed hook over the tree branches. The sloth's sluggish lifestyle requires very little effort and contrasts strongly with the speedy swinging of the monkeys and apes.

GRIPPING TAILS

A variety of rainforest animals, from tree porcupines and tree anteaters to kinkajous and woolly monkeys, have a special sort of tail for curling round branches like a hook. This is called a prehensile tail and it is most highly developed in South American monkeys. For some unknown reason, the monkeys of Africa and Southeast Asia have developed without this useful adaptation. Most monkeys with prehensile tails use them as a fifth limb, for holding and gathering their food, as well as for moving.

HAIRY SWINGER

With their long arms and strong fingers and toes, orang-utans move easily through the trees, using their feet as well as their hands for climbing. To travel fast, they swing hand over hand, a technique called 'brachiating'. Older male orangs are too heavy to do this, but females and young are adept at tree-top travel, sometimes walking along branches as well as brachiating. A female orang-utan has an armspan of about 2.4 metres (almost 8 ft) and can cover large distances quickly.

GLUED TO THE SPOT

Tree frogs, such as this red-eyed tree frog, have special pads under the toes that produce a sticky substance called mucus. Their sticky toes help them to grip wet leaves and other slippery and slimy surfaces as they climb through the trees.

FOOD CHAIN

JAGUAR

COLLARED PECCARY

GRASS, ROOTS, BULBS & WORMS

One of the many links between rainforest plants and animals is through their feeding habits. All food chains start with plants because they make their own food, and then the plant-eaters (herbivores), in turn are eaten by meat-eaters, (carnivores).

HIDDEN KILLER

Curled up among the leaves of the forest floor, the gaboon viper is well camouflaged as it waits for a tasty small animal to wander past. Then it leaps out and grabs hold of its prey in a surprise attack. Gaboon vipers kill their prey by biting it with their poisonous fangs. They have the longest fangs of any snake – each one is up to 5 cm (2 inches) long. A snake's teeth are good for holding prey, but not for chopping or chewing, so snakes swallow their prey whole.

PREDATORS & PREY

Rainforest predators are mostly small animals because there are not enough large plant-eaters in the forest to sustain large meat-eaters. The exceptions to this are the large cats, such as the jaguar and the tiger, which hunt pigs, antelope and deer on the forest floor. Ground-dwelling snakes also lie in wait for their prey on the forest floor, while their tree-dwelling relatives lurk among the branches. Other ground predators include troops of bush dogs in South America and sloth bears in southern India and Sri Lanka. High-level hunters include the fierce hawks and eagles that swoop down into the canopy to sieze monkeys and sloths in their strong talons.

TERRIBLE TEETH

Some piranha fish, such as red-bellied piranhas, are lethal killers, carving slices of flesh from their victims with razor-sharp teeth. They have powerful jaws that snap together in a strong bite. Meat-eating piranhas have been known to attack animals as large as goats, which have fallen into the water. But all piranhas live on fruit and nuts for most of the year and some are completely vegetarian.

FELINE HUNTER

Small, agile forest cats, such as this South American margay, are skilled climbers that prey on small rodents, birds and lizards in the trees. Most of them are nocturnal hunters and their yellow or brownish fur with spotted or striped markings gives them good camouflage. Keen sight, hearing and smell enable them to track down their victims, which are killed with a neck bite from their sharp, pointed teeth.

SNAPPING JAWS

The caimans of Central and South America have sharper, longer teeth than their relatives the alligators. They lurk in the water, waiting to snap up fish, frogs or thirsty animals that come down to the forest rivers for a drink. Caimans have strong, bony plates in their back and belly scales for protection against their own predators.

TONGUE ZAPPER

Insects are a major source of food for many rainforest predators, from birds and bats, to tarantula spiders and chameleons. Chameleons flick out their incredibly long tongues at lightning speed to trap insects, spiders, scorpions and other prey on the sticky tip. To search for food, a chameleon can swivel its eyes in all directions. Their movements can be so slow that they are hardly noticeable, especially since the chameleon can change colour to blend with its surroundings.

FOOD CHAIN

BENTWING BAT

INSECTS

FLOWERS

This food chain from an Australian rainforest has three links. Should any link be destroyed it will affect the rest of the chain, and all the other food chains in the large and complex food web.

DEFENCE

From armour and camouflage to weapons and poisons, rainforest animals use all kinds of defence tactics to avoid being eaten. Sometimes it is possible to run, leap, fly or glide away from a predator, but hiding or blending in with the background is often more successful. Many rainforest insects look just like leaves, twigs or bark, and as long as they keep still they are hard to detect. Certain spiders even disguise themselves as bird droppings. Poisonous animals tend to have bright warning colours to tell predators to keep away. Some non-poisonous butterflies, such as postman butterflies, copy the colours of poisonous species to trick predators. Another way animals may defend themselves is by putting up a fight.

ANGRY PIGS

The giant forest hog is the largest wild pig and is feared by forest peoples for its unpredictable temper. It has well developed lower canine teeth that stick out of the sides of the mouth to form tusks. Males have larger tusks than females.

SPIDER SURVIVAL

This tarantula is trying to make itself look as frightening as possible to scare predators away. Spiders use their poisonous fangs for defence and tarantulas also flick irritating hairs at attackers. A few spiders look just like stinging insects such as wasps or ants so predators are tricked into leaving them alone. Spiders will even pretend to be dead, since predators prefer to eat living prey.

FROG POISONS

Poison dart frogs secrete deadly poisons in their skin and are brightly coloured to warn potential predators to keep away. They make some of these poisons themselves but also obtain some from their food, such as toxic insects. Their poisons are so powerful that a tiny smear is enough to kill a horse. A few Amazonian tribes use this poison on the tips of their blowpipe darts for hunting.

HIDE AND SEEK

Insects are a major source of food in the rainforest so they have developed a huge variety of unusual colours, patterns and shapes to pretend they are not nice, tasty snacks. Dead leaves are a good disguise to adopt and leaf insects often have veins and tattered edges just like the real thing.

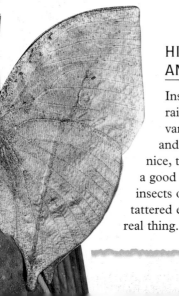

FALSE EYES

Some camouflaged butterflies and moths have a second line of defence if they are disturbed by a predator. They suddenly open their front wings to reveal bright colours (called flash colours) and markings on their back wings. The markings may look like the eyes of a rainforest cat or snake. This sudden display startles the predator, making them hesitate long enough for the butterfly or moth to escape.

BODY ARMOUR

Pangolins are protected by a covering of horny skin scales which overlap like the tiles on a roof. When the pangolin curls tightly into a ball, the scales form a tough shield which only the larger cats can bite through. Pangolins eat ants and termites and their body armour helps to protect them from insect bites and stings as well as from predators.

TREE DEFENCE

To deter leaf-eating insects, the rubber tree produces a milky latex which hardens into a sticky gum. This sticks the insects' mouthparts together and prevents them from eating the tree. This latex is the raw material for making rubber. It is collected by making slanting cuts in the bark. The latex oozes slowly from the cuts and is collected in a cup fixed to the tree trunk. The bark gradually heals and the trees can be tapped again and again over a number of years.

Night-Time Animals

As darkness falls swiftly over the rainforest, squeaks, scratchings and rustlings fill the night air. The rainforest becomes dimly lit by moonlight, flashing fireflies or glowing fungi. As much as 80 per cent of all animal activity in a rainforest takes place at night. The darkness hides animals from their enemies while the cool, moist night air suits insects and amphibians. Night-time, or nocturnal, animals live in all parts of the rainforests. Deer, okapi and armadillos roam the forest floor while tarsiers, bushbabies, bats, moths and small jungle cats move through the trees. Some flowers open up specially at night so they can be pollinated by nocturnal animals. To find their way in the dark, nocturnal animals have special senses, such as huge eyes or very sensitive ears and noses. Some snakes, called pit vipers, can pick up the heat given off by birds and mammals and use this to track their prey in the dark.

BAT TRANSPORT

Rainforest bats, such this long-tongued bat, fly through the forest at night searching for nectar, fruit and insects. As they visit the forest flowers, bats help to spread their pollen and their seeds, so the bats and the forests help each other to survive.

SLOW MOVERS

Pottos move very slowly and deliberately through the trees so their movements go undetected. If a potto hears the slightest sound or unexpected movement, it will suddenly freeze until it feels the danger has passed. It can stay 'frozen' like this for hours if necessary but the technique only works well in very thick, leafy vegetation.

NIGHT CAMOUFLAGE

The spotted markings of the clouded leopard help it to hide when it is hunting at night by breaking up the outline of its body among the leaves and branches of the forest trees. Clouded leopards hunt by pouncing from tree branches as well as by stalking prey on the ground.

TOAD INVASION

The cane toad from South America has been introduced into the rainforests of northeastern Australia. The spotted-tailed quoll (left) hunts and kills the toad but, unfortunately, is killed by the poison in the toad's skin and so the quolls' numbers have fallen drastically. The toad has no natural predators in Australia because it comes from another country, so its numbers are increasing.

NIGHT MONSTER

The rare aye-aye from Madagascar has huge ears like a bat, large eyes like an owl and a bushy tail like a squirrel. But its most scary feature is its long, spindly middle finger. This finger is very useful to the aye-aye. It listens for the sound of insect larvae moving about inside branches and tree trunks and digs them out with its creepy finger. Unlike all other primates (monkeys, apes, lemurs, bushbabies and humans), the aye-aye has claws instead of nails on its fingers and toes.

EYES & EARS

The huge, bat-like ears of the lesser bushbaby help it to track the movements of its insect prey in the darkness. Insects may even be snatched out of the air as they fly past.

The large eyes let in as much light as possible and there is a special layer called a 'tapetum' at the back of the eye to reflect light back into the eye. This is what imakes the bushbabies' eyes shine in the dark.

COURTSHIP

In most rainforests, the weather stays the same all the time, and so there are no definite breeding seasons. The timing of courtship depends more on the reproductive cycles of the animals. Some pair up for life, while others only stay together for courtship and mating. Courtship displays in many birds are noisy, colourful affairs in which male birds show off their brightly coloured feathers to impress the watching females. Females tend to have duller colours, to make them less obvious to predators when they are sitting on the nest and feeding their young. Male butterflies may be more brightly coloured than the females for similar reasons. Apart from colours and display, other ways of attracting a mate include scent and sound.

PHEASANT FEATHERS

To impress a female, the male argus pheasant spreads out his stunning wing feathers to make an enormous fan. He clears a space on the forest floor and struts up and down, calling loudly to attract a female. Argus pheasants live in the rainforests of Southeast Asia.

BUTTERFLY COLOURS

Some male and female butterflies, such as these morphos, are very different colours. The shimmering colours of the male may play a part in attracting a female, but the way the wings reflect ultra-violet light also seems to be important. Male butterflies use scents as well as colours to attract females and females seem to prefer the fittest males, the ones that are the strongest fliers.

BIRD OF PARADISE COURTSHIP DISPLAY

Some of the most spectacular courtship displays take place in the rainforests of New Guinea. Here, male birds of paradise perform elaborate displays; some even compete at communal display grounds, or leks, giving dazzling performances of colour and sound. They often remove leaves just above their display grounds, so that a spotlight of sunshine draws attention to their spectacular dance.

Male Raggiana birds of paradise display together to show off their fabulous plumes of feathers. They shriek loudly to attract attention.

COCK-OF-THE-ROCK

On a bare patch of the Amazon forest floor, the male cock-of-the-rock displays to watching females, which are drab brown colours. He shows off by leaping into the air, bobbing his head, snapping his bill and fanning out his feathers. He spreads his head crest forward so that it almost hides his bill. Females choose the males with the best display.

BOWERBIRDS

Instead of having bright, colourful feathers, male bowerbirds attract females by building an elaborate shelter, called a bower. Each bowerbird builds a different shape of bower from twigs woven together and decorated with colourful objects, such as shells, fruits, bones, pebbles, feathers, and flowers. Things thrown away by people, such as old bottle tops, sometimes end up decorating these bowers.

SMELLY MESSAGES

Female and male tigers live apart and only come together for mating. When a tigress is ready to mate, she leaves scent marks along the paths in her territory. This tigress is leaving a scented message for a male tiger by rubbing scent glands on her face against tree bark. She also roars loudly to attract the attention of nearby males.

PARROT COURTSHIP

Before they mate, most male parrots display to the females by bowing, hopping, strutting, flicking their wings and wagging their tails. They may also feed the female regurgitated food.

In many species, the brightly coloured irises of the eyes are expanded – this is called eye blazing. Most parrots are monogamous and males and females often pair for life. They reinforce the bond between them by preening each other's feathers and feeding each other.

LIFE CYCLE OF AN OWL BUTTERFLY

A butterfly goes through four stages in its life cycle: egg, caterpillar, pupa and adult. In the warm climate of a tropical rainforest, a butterfly develops quickly and may complete its whole life cycle in just a few weeks.

Ribs and tough coating on the eggs stop them from drying out.

Young caterpillars have a green skin; older ones have a brown skin. Their function is to eat and grow bigger.

Inside the pupa, the caterpillar changes into a butterfly.

The role of the adult butterfly is reproduction and dispersal.

FROG TRANSPORT

Poison dart frogs usually lay their eggs on a leaf or a small area of ground, which they have carefully cleaned. One or both parents visit or guard the eggs until they hatch into tadpoles. Then the parent encourages the tadpoles to wriggle up on to its back and carries them to a stream or a pool of water among the leaves of a forest plant. Up to 35 tadpoles are carried in this way. The tadpoles do not fall off the adult's back because they are held there by a sticky secretion that is only broken down when it is under water.

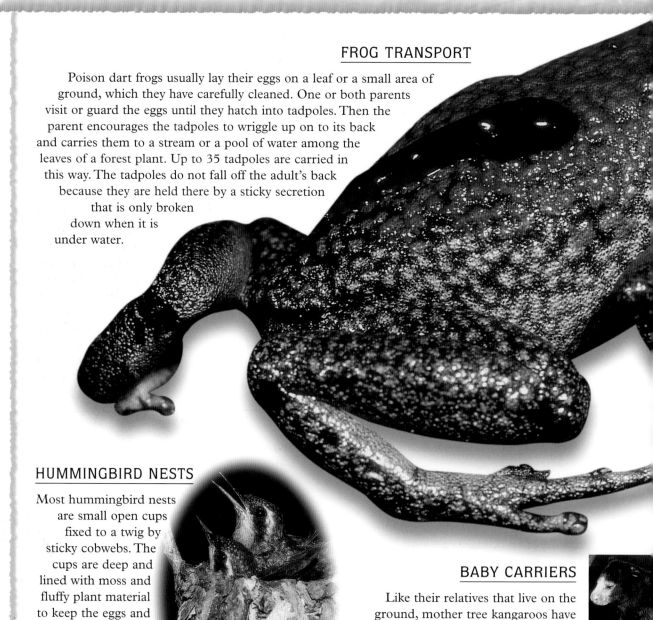

HUMMINGBIRD NESTS

Most hummingbird nests are small open cups fixed to a twig by sticky cobwebs. The cups are deep and lined with moss and fluffy plant material to keep the eggs and young birds warm. Even after leaving the nest, the fledgling hummingbird is fed by its mother for as long as 20-40 days.

BABY CARRIERS

Like their relatives that live on the ground, mother tree kangaroos have pouches to carry their young. The babies are born at a very early stage of their development. They crawl up to the pouch and fasten on to a teat to feed. Inside the pouch, the baby is warm and safe and can feed whenever it is hungry. It will spend several months there, completing its development.

NESTS, EGGS & YOUNG

Although there is plenty of food and a variety of places to nest in a rainforest, animals still have to compete for safe nesting sites and protect their eggs and young from predators. The warm temperatures help the young to develop and survive the early, vulnerable stages of the life cycle but the constant rain can make life miserable. Birds protect their eggs and young inside nests or tree holes, while marsupial mothers, such as tree kangaroos or possums, carry their young around with them for months in furry pouches. Even tarantulas guard their eggs until they hatch. But mammals, such as monkeys, cats and bats, take the greatest care of their young, teaching them how to feed, hunt and survive in the forest.

STRIPES & SPOTS

Adult Brazilian tapirs are a plain brown colour but their young have spots and stripes on their fur. This helps to camouflage them so they blend into the background as they move through the light and shade of the rainforest. The markings also break up the outline of the young animal's body so it is harder to see.

CLINGING BABIES

A female orang-utan usually gives birth to a single baby every three to six years. The baby rides on its mother's back or clings to her fur as she swings through the trees and sleeps in the same nest at night. Baby orang-utans are totally dependent on their mothers for the first 18 months of their lives. Mother orang-utans do not mate again until their young are at least three years old so a female may only have two or three babies during her lifetime.

LIVING TOGETHER

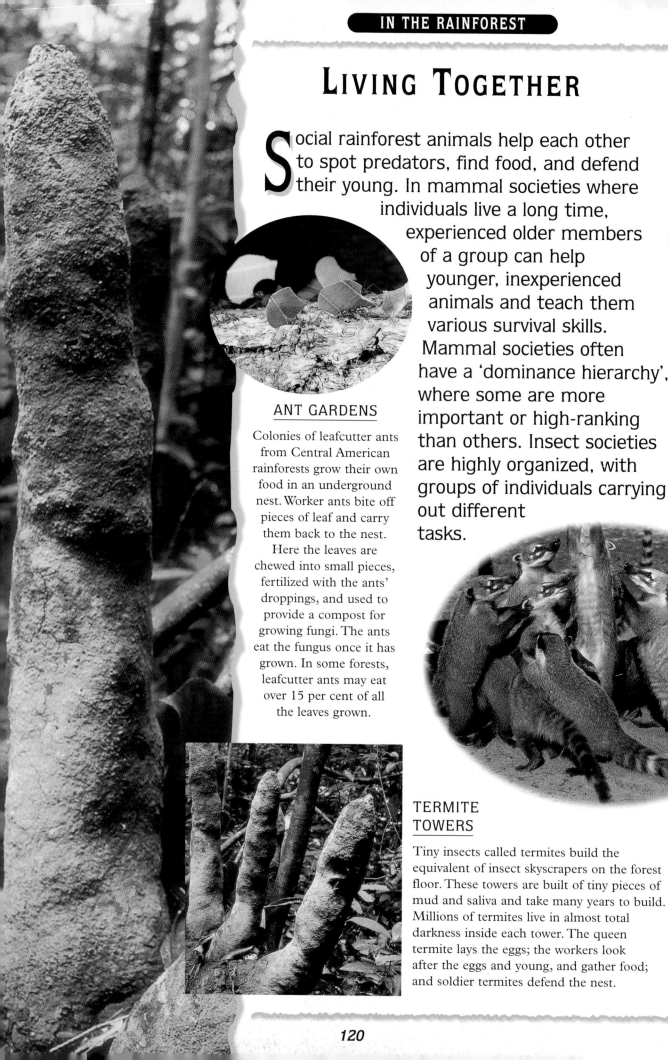

Social rainforest animals help each other to spot predators, find food, and defend their young. In mammal societies where individuals live a long time, experienced older members of a group can help younger, inexperienced animals and teach them various survival skills. Mammal societies often have a 'dominance hierarchy', where some are more important or high-ranking than others. Insect societies are highly organized, with groups of individuals carrying out different tasks.

ANT GARDENS

Colonies of leafcutter ants from Central American rainforests grow their own food in an underground nest. Worker ants bite off pieces of leaf and carry them back to the nest. Here the leaves are chewed into small pieces, fertilized with the ants' droppings, and used to provide a compost for growing fungi. The ants eat the fungus once it has grown. In some forests, leafcutter ants may eat over 15 per cent of all the leaves grown.

TERMITE TOWERS

Tiny insects called termites build the equivalent of insect skyscrapers on the forest floor. These towers are built of tiny pieces of mud and saliva and take many years to build. Millions of termites live in almost total darkness inside each tower. The queen termite lays the eggs; the workers look after the eggs and young, and gather food; and soldier termites defend the nest.

FRUIT BATS

Many species of fruit bat roost together in groups of hundreds of individuals on trees or in caves. This rousettus fruit bat is roosting in a cave on the island of Bali in Southeast Asia. At first, young bats travel with their mother all the time, but later they stay behind in the roost while she goes out to hunt.

GORILLA GROUPS

Wandering slowly through the lowland and mountain forests of central Africa, are small groups of gorillas, led by a dominant male. Mature male gorillas have silvery grey hair on their backs and are called 'silverbacks'. They are too big and heavy to climb trees, but females and young are more agile and able to climb up among the branches. Male gorillas defend the group from danger but gorillas are intelligent, peaceful animals and all the members of a group play with the young.

GIRL POWER

In Central and South America, female and young coatis roam the forests in groups of up to 20 animals. They probe holes and cracks in the ground or in the trees searching for insects, spiders and fruit. For most of the year, the adult males live alone but are allowed to join the group for the few weeks of the mating period. Even then, the males are less important in the group than the females. After mating, the females soon drive the males away.

SOUND SIGNALS

Gibbons, such as this siamang gibbon, live in monogamous family groups. The adult pair in a group utter loud and complex calls, mainly as duets. These beautiful and haunting calls help to develop and maintain pair bonds and keep neighbouring groups from invading each other's territories. Siamang gibbons stay very close to each other all the time.

PEOPLE OF THE RAINFOREST

NEW GUINEA PEOPLES

The New Guinea highlanders decorate themselves in magnificent costumes for special occasions and perform complicated dances. They paint their faces and bodies in vivid colours. The pattern often has something to do with religious beliefs and ancestral spirits.

For thousands of years, the world's rainforests have been home to groups of people who have a deep and sensitive understanding of the forests. Their knowledge of the rainforest's plants and animals, and their ability to use a wide range of foods and natural medicines, are the key to their survival but population densities have never been high. Some rainforest peoples cultivate small patches of forest in a form of shifting cultivation. Unfortunately, as forests are cleared for their timber or their land, the homes of forest peoples are destroyed, or they are killed by diseases, such as influenza and measles, introduced by settlers from outside the forest.

HUNTING WEAPONS

This Mentawai man from Indonesia is carrying his bow and arrow along with some stripped bark. To capture monkeys, birds and other prey high in the canopy, rainforest hunter-gatherers use poisoned arrows or darts. The poisons he uses come from plant juices or the skin of poisonous tree frogs, and sometimes hunters have to wait for hours before the animal dies and falls out of the trees.

PYGMIES

The Pygmies of Africa are adapted physically as well as culturally to their way of life as hunter-gatherers in the forest. Their small size makes it easier to move about in the undergrowth and they have a light muscular build which is well suited to tree climbing. Some tribes of pygmies seem to be completely at home in the tree tops, often climbing to reach the nests of wild bees to collect the honey. A small bird called a honeyguide often leads the hunters to a hive. The hunter helps the bird by opening the hive and leaves it a meal of beeswax as a reward.

NUMBERS OF PEOPLE

A large area of rainforest can support only a few hundred people – the population density of the Mbuit pygmies is only about one person for every 4 square kilometres (1.5 square miles), and an individual band may range over as much as 1,300 square kilometres (500 square miles) in their search for food. So rainforest peoples are spread thinly through the forest. Some build houses to settle for a time; many families may live in the same house.

FOREST TRANSPORT

In dense forest, it is easier to travel along rivers than to move through the undergrowth. Dugout canoes are often used for transport, even today, but making them takes a long time. A tree has to be felled and then cut and hollowed out with an axe. Pieces of wood called stretchers are placed across the canoe to prevent it warping. When the canoe is finished, a fire is lit underneath and inside the canoe to harden and seal the wood.

SHIFTING CULTIVATION

Also called 'slash-and-burn', shifting cultivation is well suited to the poor soils of a rainforest. The people cut down and burn a small area of forest so the nutrients in the plants enrich the soil for a while and weeds are destroyed. Then they plant seeds, and as the crops grow, the plot needs constant weeding, since weeds grow well in the warm, wet conditions. Eventually, the weeds overcome the crops and the goodness in the soil is used up so the people move on to another patch of forest. Cultivated areas are left to lie fallow (rest and recover), for between 8 and 20 years. Shifting cultivation does not cause any lasting harm to the forest.

CEREMONIES

Many rainforest peoples paint their bodies with colourful dyes and use feathers, flowers and other natural materials to make jewellery. Men, such as this Cofan Indian from Ecuador, are sometimes the only ones allowed to wear full ceremonial costume. There are strong traditions of dance and ceremony and special occasions such as weddings, funerals and harvests are marked by dances and feasts.

PROTECTING THE RAINFOREST

Rainforests have taken millions of years to turn into the complex environments that they are today. They are very fragile because every part depends on every other part. Unfortunately, most rainforests are in poor, developing countries, which need to make money from timber, mineral resources, such as iron, copper or uranium, or cash-crops, such as coffee, cocoa or bananas. Forest clearance causes many problems such as soil erosion, floods, droughts, extinction of species and disturbance of forest peoples. About half of all the rainforests in the world have already been cut down and an area about the size of a soccer pitch disappears every second. Much more could be done to save the world's rainforests. Timber companies could replace the trees they cut down, or grow plantations of valuable rainforest trees. Trade in rare animal species could be controlled more effectively, and more large areas of rainforest preserved as national parks.

TIMBER!

With chain saws, diggers and powerful machinery, logging companies can clear huge areas of rainforest in a frighteningly short time. It takes several hundred years for a rainforest tree to grow taller than an electricity pylon and only a few minutes for a man to chop it down with a chainsaw. Roads have to be built to get the machinery into the forest and, as the valuable timber trees are scattered throughout the forest, great holes have to be torn in the forest to reach each one. Loggers usually destroy three times as many trees as they harvest.

OUT INTO THE WILD

The numbers of endangered species can be increased by breeding them in captivity and then releasing them back into the wild. This is not a simple process as the animals have never been in a natural rainforest and have to learn how to survive. Scientists have fitted these tamarins with radio collars so they can follow their movements through the forest. In 1908, only about 100 golden lion tamarins survived in the wild, but conservation work has now increased numbers to about 400.

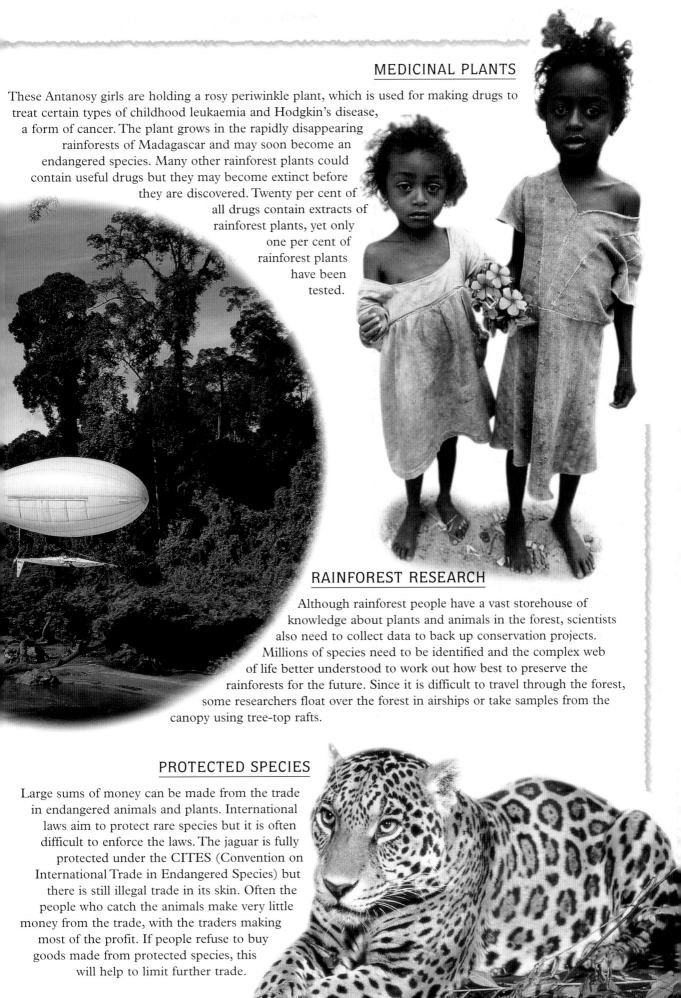

MEDICINAL PLANTS

These Antanosy girls are holding a rosy periwinkle plant, which is used for making drugs to treat certain types of childhood leukaemia and Hodgkin's disease, a form of cancer. The plant grows in the rapidly disappearing rainforests of Madagascar and may soon become an endangered species. Many other rainforest plants could contain useful drugs but they may become extinct before they are discovered. Twenty per cent of all drugs contain extracts of rainforest plants, yet only one per cent of rainforest plants have been tested.

RAINFOREST RESEARCH

Although rainforest people have a vast storehouse of knowledge about plants and animals in the forest, scientists also need to collect data to back up conservation projects. Millions of species need to be identified and the complex web of life better understood to work out how best to preserve the rainforests for the future. Since it is difficult to travel through the forest, some researchers float over the forest in airships or take samples from the canopy using tree-top rafts.

PROTECTED SPECIES

Large sums of money can be made from the trade in endangered animals and plants. International laws aim to protect rare species but it is often difficult to enforce the laws. The jaguar is fully protected under the CITES (Convention on International Trade in Endangered Species) but there is still illegal trade in its skin. Often the people who catch the animals make very little money from the trade, with the traders making most of the profit. If people refuse to buy goods made from protected species, this will help to limit further trade.

INDEX

fishing 92, 93
flash floods 9
flying fish 70, 73
flying lizard 108
forest clearance 124
forest hog 112
foxes 4, 6
   Arctic 51, 52, 54, 55
   desert 16, 17, 25, 29
frill-necked lizard 27
frogs 28, 97, 109, 112, 118
fruit bats 96, 121
fungi 114, 120

G
gaboon vipers 110
Galapagos penguins 85
garden eels 73
gecko 17
geese 44
gemsbok 30
George River herd
   caribou 61
giant anteaters 97
giant clams 83
giant millipedes 97
giant petrels 53
gibbons 121
Gibraltar, Strait of 68
Gila monster lizard 15, 35
glass jellyfish 78
Glaucus (sea slug) 84
gliders 101, 108
global warming 64
goats 7
Gobi Desert 10, 15, 32
golden moles 25
goliath beetle 102
goliath frog 97
goose barnacles 91
gorillas 121
grass 110
Great Barrier Reef 83
Great Basin Desert 10
Great Bear constellation
   40
Great Sandy Desert 10
Great Victoria Desert
   10, 32
Greenland 38, 40
grey parrots 102
ground squirrels 26
Gulf Stream 68
gulper eel 76

H
hairgrass 41
hares 4, 51, 52
hatchet fish 75

hawks 24, 110
hermit crab 91
herring 73
hoatzin 105
hogs 97, 112
   see also pigs
honey ants 31
honeyguides 122
Hopi 32
hornbills 102
horned vipers 21
howler monkeys 96
Humboldt Current 8
hummingbirds 118
humpback whales 67
hurricanes 103
huskies 36, 38
hyenas 25

I, J
ice 40, 41, 69
ice fish 48, 49
igloos 62
Indian Ocean 68, 69
insects
   Arctic 39, 43, 44
   desert 28, 30
   rainforest 96, 111, 112
Inuit 62
irrigation schemes 35
isopods 46-7
jack rabbits 21, 26
jaguars 97, 110, 125
jellyfish 72, 78
jerboa 17
jungle see rainforest
jungle cats 114

K
Kaafu Atol, Maldives 69
Kalahari Desert 10, 32
Kalapolo Indians 97
kangaroo rats 16
kangaroos 18, 101, 118, 119
kelp 81
killer whales 53, 60, 85
king penguins 57
kingsnake 25
kinkajous 108
Kolmanskop 9
krill 53, 65

L
Lapps 63
Las Vegas 35
leafcutter ants 120
lemmings 44, 45, 53, 55
lemurs 97
leopard seals 52

lichens 42, 99
lionfish 83, 84
little auks 45
lizards
   desert 15, 17, 28
   endangered 35
   predators 24, 27
   survival 20, 21
   young 28
lobsters 72
locusts 14, 25
loggerhead turtles 88

M
mackerel 73
magnetic pole 37
Malayan tapir 100
mangrove forests 98, 99, 100
manta ray 73
margay 110
Mariana Trench 70
marine nature reserves
   95
marlin 67
marsupials 11, 101, 119
   see also named species
Mbuit pygmies 123
medicinal plants 125
Mediterranean 68
meerkats 28
Mentawai 122
mermaid's purses 88
mice 6, 11, 16, 25
Mid-Atlantic Ridge 68
midges 46-7
migration 44, 48, 50-1
minerals 76, 124
mining 92
mites 47
Mojave Desert 10
molluscs 72
moloch lizard 25
monkeys 5, 96, 102, 103, 121
   movement 108
   predators 110
   and seed distribution 106
   young 119
   see also named species
monsoon forests 99
Monument Valley 10
Morocco 33
morpho butterflies 103, 116
mosquitoes 44
mosses 42
moths 30, 100, 107, 114
mucus 109
musk oxen 55, 56, 61

N
Namaqualand 23
Namib Desert 6, 10, 13, 19, 34
Namibia 9
narwhals 56, 60
Navajo 32
Nenets 62, 63
Nevada Desert 35
New Guinea highlanders
   122
nomads 7
North Pole 4, 36, 37, 40
nunataks 41

O
oases 13, 33
oceans 5, 66-95
   abyss 70
   creatures 66, 67, 84-91
   dark zone 70, 71
   deep 71, 76, 77, 78, 79
   people 92, 93
   plants 67, 80, 81
   protection 94, 95
   sunlit zone 70, 71, 72, 73
   trenches 70
   twilight zone 70, 74, 75
   see also coral reefs
oil 35, 64, 65, 92
okapi 114
opals 32
orang-utan 109, 119
orchids 99, 106
oryx 30
owl butterflies 118
owls 6, 16, 53, 58
ozone layer 65

P
Pacific Ocean 68, 69, 70
palm trees 33
pangolins 113
parasitic plants 105
parrot fish 73
parrots 102, 117
pearls 93
pearlwort Colobanthus
   41
peccaries 31, 97, 110
penguins 4, 37, 46, 47, 60
   breeding 57, 58, 59
   and cold 49
   movement 50
   predators 53, 54, 85
permafrost 8
petrels 46
Philodendron 107